Who has woe? Who has sorrow?
  Who has strife? Who has complaints?
  Who has needless bruises? Who has bloodshot eyes?
Those who linger over wine,
  who go to sample bowls of mixed wine.
Do not gaze at wine when it is red,
  when it sparkles in the cup,
  when it goes down smoothly!
In the end it bites like a snake
  and poisons like a viper.
Your eyes will see strange sights
  and your mind imagine confusing things.
You will be like one sleeping on the high seas,
  lying on top of the rigging.
"They hit me," you will say, "but I'm not hurt!
  They beat me, but I don't feel it!
When will I wake up
  so I can find another drink?"

PROVERBS 23:29-35

Still Married, Still Sober

HOPE for Your Alcoholic Marriage

DAVID & ELSIE MACKENZIE
with Beth Spring

Foreword by John Guest

INTERVARSITY PRESS
DOWNERS GROVE, ILLINOIS 60515

InterVarsity Press is the book-publishing division of InterVarsity Christian Fellowship, a student movement active on campus at hundreds of universities, colleges and schools of nursing in the United States of America, and a member movement of the International Fellowship of Evangelical Students. For information about local and regional activities, write Public Relations Dept., InterVarsity Christian Fellowship, 6400 Schroeder Rd., P.O. Box 7895, Madison, WI 53707-7895.

All Scripture quotations, unless otherwise indicated, are from the Holy Bible, New International Version. Copyright 1973, 1978, International Bible Society. Used by permission of Zondervan Bible Publishers.

Cover illustration: Photo by Beth Spring; tinting by Gary Guidovic

ISBN 0-8308-1376-4

Printed in the United States of America ∞

Library of Congress Cataloging-in-Publication Data
MacKenzie, David (David C.)
      Still married, still sober: hope for your alcoholic marriage/
   David and Elsie MacKenzie, with Beth Spring.
         p.   cm.
      Includes bibliographical references.
      ISBN 0-8308-1376-4
      1. Alcoholics—United States—Family relationships.   2. Marriage—
   United States.   3. Alcoholics—Rehabilitation—United States.
   I. MacKenzie, Elsie.   II. Spring, Beth.   III. Title.
   HV5132.M33   1991
   362.29'23—dc20   *91-21963*
                                                                                      CIP

15	14	13	12	11	10	9	8	7	6	5	4	3	2	1
03	02	01	00	99	98	97	96	95	94	93	92	91		

To Diane Gordon MacKenzie
1887-1973
"Gamie"
She always prayed
and never lost faith.

Foreword

During a series of evangelistic meetings, I told the story of Dave and Elsie MacKenzie's struggle with alcoholism, their divorce and remarriage. A short while later, a woman came to see me. She had been listening to the series of talks on her car radio, and when she heard about the MacKenzies she made her way straight to the hall where the meetings were being held. "If there is hope for a marriage like the one you described," she said, "then there is hope for my marriage as well."

Hope for marriages ravaged by alcoholism is the message of this book. It's a message Dave and Elsie have shared with audiences throughout the United States and during a trip to Australia with me. They are living examples of the power of the Holy Spirit at work today in lives and marriages on the brink of destruction.

Today all of us are influenced by the ease with which couples opt for divorce. Particularly when alcoholism is involved, the rationale for divorce may seem utterly compelling, even to a Christian husband or wife. Dave and Elsie send a different message—one that stands squarely opposed to our present divorce-oriented culture.

In 1972 when Dave and Elsie told me they planned to recommit their lives to one another as husband and wife, I suggested they do so publicly to give glory to God. They agreed, and they were remarried during a Sunday morning worship service. In the same spirit of openness, honesty and compassion for others Dave and Elsie have written a warm and practical book especially for people who long to salvage their marriages, homes and children from the death grip of alcoholism.

John Guest

CHAPTER 1

Alcoholic & Married

The morning after their 1966 wedding in Sewickley, *Pennsylvania, Dave and Elsie MacKenzie were heading west in a brand-new, hunter-green Mustang—a wedding gift from Elsie's parents. The honeymoon had to be postponed because Elsie was scheduled to have surgery in a week, so they were driving to their first home, in Michigan City, Indiana.*

Dave reached behind the driver's seat, groping for a stashed six-pack of beer. He loosened one can from the cardboard carrier, reached into the glove compartment for an opener, and punched two holes in the top of the can. The aroma filled the car as he began drinking. In minutes the can was empty. And not too many minutes later, he reached for another can.

Elsie remembers a momentary shiver of fear as she watched

him. "Honey, are you going to drink while you're driving?" she asked. Dave replied with characteristic breezy self-confidence. "Yeah, I'll just have a couple."

About halfway through the eight-hour drive—and more than halfway through the six-pack—they passed a serious accident. One car was in flames and several others askew along the road's shoulder. Elsie's new-bride deference flew right out the window. "Pull over now, Dave. I'm going to drive."

Reluctantly, Dave stopped the car. Less than five miles down the highway, he was sound asleep as Elsie gripped the wheel and reassured herself. "He needed to unwind after all the excitement of the wedding," she rationalized. "This heavy beer drinking is just a holdover from college. He won't keep it up now that he's married."

That evening, Dave and Elsie moved into their new apartment. Elsie's anxieties about Dave's drinking and driving receded as she began organizing her kitchen, but alcohol reappeared like an unwelcome drop-in guest the next day. Dave went to work as a management trainee at a manufacturing company. He called and told Elsie that there was a softball game scheduled after work, and he wanted to play. "Afterwards, all the guys have a few beers at the tavern that sponsors our team," he told Elsie. "I'll be home around 9 P.M."

Elsie busily and happily immersed herself in unpacking boxes, cleaning the apartment and setting up the home she'd been dreaming of. She scarcely noticed when 9 P.M. came and went—with no Dave.

By 10 P.M., Elsie was exhausted. She sat on the sofa, thumbed through a magazine and eyed the door, anticipating Dave's return. Another hour passed. The shudder of fear she'd *felt the day before in the car gripped her again. As she sat and worried about her husband, the fear grew into a full-fledged panic attack.*

Images of car wrecks, a barroom brawl or a bizarre disappearance plagued Elsie as she paced the tiny apartment. She did not know how to cope with her sudden sense of desperation because she had no previous experience with problem drinking and its unsettling effects. She grew up in a warm, loving home with a father who was steady, dependable and considerate. At the tender age of twenty-three, she had no internal compass to tell her what to do now.

And there was something else. Elsie had known Dave for a little more than a year. Suddenly she wondered: How well did she really know him? Doubts stabbed at her as she recalled several occasions throughout their brief courtship when Dave drank too much. Elsie had pretended not to notice, but others (even her father) would point it out. Now, those voices chorused their warnings in her mind, and she recalled Dave's devil-may-care attitude about drinking beer while he drove. Eventually, she worked herself into a frenzy, venting her rage on her newly organized cupboards, scattering their contents and hurling pots and pans against the floor.

By midnight, spent, Elsie yanked open their Murphy bed from out of the living room wall and tore the bed coverings off it. She dragged a blanket into the bathroom and curled up in the bathtub, sobbing.

An hour later, Dave lurched through the door. He steadied himself with one hand against the wall and gaped in puzzlement at the disheveled room.

Elsie stalked out of the bathroom, tensed and angry but keeping her distance from her 6'4" drunken husband. "Where were you?" she demanded. "Don't you remember you were supposed to be home at nine?" Fully expecting an apology, a hug, a hint of concern about her feelings, Elsie was amazed when Dave attacked her verbally. He acted as if he hadn't even heard her questions.

"Look what you've done," he yelled. "You've torn the place apart. What's your problem? You knew I'd come home!"

The verbal blasting subsided quickly. Although Dave had not hit or slapped Elsie, a fresh, painful wound throbbed inside her for the rest of the night. Her emotions reeled with hurt, surprise, fury and a nagging question: Is this what marriage is like?

By morning, after a fitful sleep, life looked a bit brighter. Dave was up and dressed and headed for the office again. Elsie consoled herself as she tidied the apartment and wrote a grocery list. "He's just acting like a college guy," she said to herself. "It won't happen again."

This incident is one of many we wish we could erase from the history of our marriage. It hurts to recall even now, more than two decades later, just how often Dave's drinking pushed our marriage to the limits of its endurance. The pattern established just after our wedding persisted and grew steadily worse for over three years. Eventually, as Dave plunged further into alcohol addiction, we divorced.

We both believed that our life together was over—a sorry last chapter to a story best forgotten entirely. Yet God had a different plan. Two-and-one-half years after our divorce, profound changes were apparent. Dave was sober and actively involved in alcoholism recovery circles. We both committed our lives to the Lord and began seeking his will for our future. To our astonishment, God's plan included reconciliation and remarriage.

Most marriages racked by alcoholism do not have such a storybook ending, and even when reconciliation happens, the pain and problems don't stop at once. In our pain we learned an important lesson: God uses our weakness to demonstrate his strength. Instead of erasing the ravages of alcoholism in our marriage—instead of rewinding it magically like a videotape to begin again—God has allowed us to use the most painful and embarrassing aspects of our story to touch other marriages crippled by alcoholism.

Today, Dave is rector of St. Christopher's Episcopal Church in Portsmouth, Virginia. Elsie stays home with two teenaged daughters. Together, we have counseled many spouses seeking help for themselves and an alcoholic loved one.

The stories we hear repeatedly sound remarkably like our own. All too often, the nonalcoholic spouse is just as naive as Elsie was in those early days and just as reticent to come to grips with the problem and seek help. In American society "alcoholism" brings to mind a cluster of unpleasant images. There is the street person idling near liquor stores and the bar patron stumbling home late at night. Practically all the images associated with alcoholism have to do with individuals, usually men, who are isolated and distinctly awful to be around.

Yet alcoholism is a family affair. Some experts say there are as many as 26 million alcoholics in America. If one of them belongs to your family, you may be just as confused and enraged as Elsie was. You may hope your alcoholic will "snap out of it" or "straighten up." If you *are* an alcoholic, you may harbor the same wrong notions about your drinking. What you may not know are the facts about alcoholism and the extent to which it affects everyone close to the alcoholic. It's not only the one drinking who needs help!

If alcoholism is intruding upon your marriage, you already know how cruel, destructive and insidious it can be. You may have done some reading about alcoholism, and you've probably heard of Alcoholics Anonymous (AA) and groups such as Al-Anon and Alateen. Those resources are excellent, and you will learn more about them in this book. At the same time, however, you may be wondering how your marriage can survive.

Frequently, marriage counselors and therapists are poorly informed about alcoholism recovery. Also, AA and similar groups focus their excellent work primarily on individuals, not relationships. That is why this book is being written. We seek to build a bridge between successful alcoholism recovery and successful marriage relationships. Based on our own experience, we believe there is hope for marriages threatened by alcoholism.

Seeking Help
Alcohol treatment and recovery programs are successful when the alcoholic gets serious about living differently and when he or she has sufficient support and encouragement from loved ones. That happens best in the environment of a stable marriage.

Some years ago, the theory was that alcoholics had to "hit bottom" before treatment could begin successfully. It was assumed that only when alcoholics reached a point of extreme degradation would they be motivated enough to complete a treatment program successfully. That is no longer thought to be the case. Letting the alcoholic hit bottom is dangerous, because at the bottom lurks the finality of divorce or suicide.

Today, better paths to an alcoholic's recovery are recognized—paths that do not include a downward spiral toward self-destruction. Before your marriage collapses, before alcohol tightens its grip any further, there are steps you can take *right now* to stop the deadly progress of the disease and its effects.

One of those steps is to seek counseling from a professional who understands alcoholism. In our experience more than half the people who visit Dave for pastoral marital counseling are coping with a drinking problem. Let's listen in on a typical counseling session in his office, with a woman we will call "Christine."

Christine is in her early thirties, college-educated and, to all outward appearances, very successful. She and her husband, Bill, own a home, one car and a minivan; they have a two-year-old daughter. Christine comes to church regularly, but Bill doesn't. I've only met him twice—at social functions. Both times he appeared to be drinking too much, so as Christine speaks I stay alert for signals that suggest a drinking problem.

"I need to talk to you," Christine says, clutching her purse on her lap. "We're having trouble in our marriage." I ask her to describe this "trouble."

"Well, Bill and I don't talk to each other very much any more. He seems more and more distant," Christine explains. "And we never go out together. He still goes out with his friends, or even by himself, and he likes to stay out late."

"Does your husband enjoy drinking when he's out?" I ask her. It's a simple, nonthreatening question, yet Christine reacts defensively.

"Sure, he likes to drink . . . but just on weekends . . . and just to relax a little. His job is so demanding, and the people at work don't appreciate him. He only drinks to cope with the stress."

"Do you mind if I ask you some questions about Bill's drinking habits?" Christine grows visibly uncomfortable, but indicates that she is willing to keep talking. I ask her about three aspects of her husband's alcohol consumption:

1. Does he tend to continue drinking after others have stopped or until he is drunk? (For some people, "social drinking" is not possible. They do not choose to drink; their bodies tell them they must drink.)

2. Do you notice any personality changes in him after he's been drinking? In other words, how does alcohol affect him?

3. Is there a history of drinking problems in his family?

Christine considers each question, one at a time. After his evenings out with his friends, she reports, Bill is invariably drunk. Christine says she doesn't even know what time he comes home most Friday and Saturday nights. There he is the next morning, passed out on the living room sofa—or floor.

Is he a different person after he's been drinking? Christine mulls over this question carefully. "I am just not sure I know him anymore," she says. "The Bill I married was so genuine, really committed to making our marriage work. Now he doesn't seem to take care of himself, and he certainly doesn't care about my needs."

Christine is crying softly, so I pass a box of tissues to her and stop asking questions. I say:

Let me tell you something about myself. I am an alcoholic, and I have been in Alcoholics Anonymous for twenty years.

Being an alcoholic means there is something different about my body that does not metabolize alcohol the way regular people do. It's a condition that cannot be cured; but it can be controlled. It means I can't drink—period. It's akin to an allergy: If I broke out with hives every time I ate asparagus, I would no longer eat asparagus.

Christine ventures a smile. She didn't expect a graying Episcopal priest to crack a joke.

I tell her how incredibly easy it is to deny that any drinking problem exists. I knew I had a serious drinking problem when I graduated from college, yet I successfully hid the extent of my drinking from Elsie until after we were married. I tell Christine about that first dreadful evening in Michigan City when Elsie and I were newlyweds. I explain:

What happened that night was so typical of those early married years, and so typical of what alcoholics go through. One after another, each of the guys at the bar would say, "Well, it's time to be getting home," and they'd leave. I kept saying exactly the same thing: "Well, I need to be home by 9 P.M." Yet for some reason, I remained glued to my barstool, drinking and drinking.

Soon, everyone would be gone, and the bar would be closing. I knew, even before our marriage was one day old, that I was out of control. And I was hurting our relationship. I felt just the way St. Paul must have felt when he wrote his letter to the Romans. I did exactly those things that I didn't want to do, and I could not do the good things

I intended. To say the least, it was frightening.

I've been droning on for several minutes now, while Christine composes herself. She is looking at me intently ... puzzled. "Are you telling me Bill is an alcoholic? He's my husband, we have a baby girl at home. And he has so many plans for the future—he wants to open his own business someday. He can't possibly be an alcoholic!"

Understanding Alcoholism

No one sets out to become an alcoholic—neither Bill nor any other husband and father, wife and mother, or adolescent. What happens is this: While most people can decide for themselves whether to have a second glass of wine or a third beer, an alcoholic cannot. Alcohol is not a universally addictive drug like heroin or crack cocaine. It only makes addicts out of people who for some reason are physically susceptible to it.

It is crucial to understand the difference between alcohol addiction and alcohol abuse. Anyone can abuse alcohol by drinking too much, but that doesn't mean he or she is an alcoholic. The difference has to do with choice. The abuser chooses to abuse. The alcoholic finds he does not have a choice after the first drink; he is compelled to keep drinking.

Alcoholism is a complicated phenomenon because it has clear physical, emotional and spiritual dimensions. Physically, the alcoholic deteriorates and experiences a progression of harmful symptoms. These are detailed in chapter four.

Emotionally, alcoholics fail to mature. The way in which we mature is by facing and resolving problems—learning to do things differently next time. Alcoholics avoid problems and never deal with them. They just get drunk. Spiritually, alcoholics experience increasing separation from God and other people as their dependence on alcohol grows. Guilt and shame wash over them, along with a deep sense of persisting in sin. As an alcoholic, trying to reconcile the ideal of who I want to be with the reality of who I am sends me fleeing from God and other people.

If you suspect your spouse is an alcoholic, you already know that problem drinking can devastate a marriage. Before your relationship deteriorates past a point of no return, what can you do?

The first step involves learning the facts about alcohol and alcoholism. The following true/false test will give you a chance to test your knowledge. You will find the correct answers explained in the appendix.

True or False?

1. Alcohol is predominantly a sedative or depressant drug.

2. Alcohol has the same chemical and physiological effect on everyone who drinks.

3. Alcohol is an addictive drug, and anyone who drinks long and hard enough will become addicted.

4. When the alcoholic is drinking, he reveals his true personality.

5. People become alcoholics because they have psychological or emotional problems that they try to relieve by drinking.

6. All sorts of social problems—marriage problems, a death in the family, job stress—may cause alcoholism.

7. If people would only drink responsibly, they would not become alcoholics.

8. Addiction to alcohol is often psychological.

9. Psychotherapy can help many alcoholics achieve sobriety through self-understanding.

10. An alcoholic has to want help to be helped.

11. Some alcoholics can learn to drink normally and can continue to drink with no ill effects as long as they limit the amount.

12. Tranquilizers and sedatives are sometimes useful in treating alcoholics.

Charting a New Course

Couples such as Christine and Bill are fortunate, though they may not yet realize it. Unlike some spouses we counsel, these two are not yet at the brink of divorce. Bill can be helped. He might recover, and the marriage might well survive. It will not be easy, however. And it will take time.

Alcoholism tightens its grip on its victims at different rates. Some people are addicted almost instantaneously; for others, it is a long, slow progression. Some become "maintenance" drinkers, sipping alcohol almost continuously to preserve the effect. Other alcoholics are "binge" drinkers, as Dave was.

In either case being married to an alcoholic and covering up for him or her is a terribly difficult way of life. The stress of living a lie finally sets in, and the nonalcoholic spouse may flee in anger or seek help . . . sometimes both.

When someone comes to us who is clearly ready to file for divorce, we counsel the person to postpone the decision and reconsider. Generally, if a spouse is hurt and angry enough to seek counseling, then that person still loves the alcoholic.

We tell them:

You can quit being married. That may appear to be the

best way out, but it won't make life perfect for you. There may be a heavy emotional price to pay later. Your other choice is to work on your marriage ... help your spouse overcome this, as only a spouse can help.

If the nonalcoholic spouse feels there is a threat of physical abuse or violence in the home—if a wife, for example, is being beaten or otherwise harmed by her alcoholic husband—then separating is the right thing to do. To remove herself physically from his presence might in fact be the best thing ever to happen to an alcoholic husband. Once she is gone, who will telephone the boss with an excuse for his tardiness in the morning? Who will make certain his clothing is clean and pressed? Who will prevent him from behaving like a fool at the neighborhood cook-out?

This approach—separation without divorce—is often an appropriate step to take when one spouse needs to exercise "tough love." In James Dobson's book *Love Must Be Tough,* he addresses the unique problems faced by the spouse of an alcoholic. Endorsing the support that can be gained from Alcoholics Anonymous and its sister organization for family members, Al-Anon, Dobson writes that separation may be necessary "until the victim [of alcoholism] is so miserable that his denial will no longer hold up."[1]

Why God Hates Divorce

When people come to us for counsel, they generally have at least some sensitivity to spiritual issues. Usually, they are regular churchgoers, if not personally committed believers. In any event, we ask them, "Why do you suppose God so dislikes divorce?" (His laws are in place for a reason, and the Bible makes it crystal clear that divorce should not be contemplated nearly as often as it is today.)

"So guard yourself in your spirit, and do not break faith with the wife of your youth. 'I hate divorce,' says the LORD God of Israel" (Mal 2:15-16). So wrote the prophet Malachi. In 1 Corinthians 7, Paul offers a wealth of advice regarding marriage. In characteristically direct terms, he advises, "A wife must not separate from her husband. But if she does, she must remain unmarried or else be reconciled to her husband. And a husband must not divorce his wife" (vv. 10-11).

For those who have committed their lives to God, divorce is an extreme last resort. In almost every case, it precludes reconciliation. There are two principles of marriage that help illustrate why divorce is wrong. They also form the basis of new perceptions about marriage that the nonalcoholic spouse can test against the realities of current home life.

The first is bonding. God's intention and purpose for creating humankind male and female, according to Genesis chapter one and reiterated by Jesus in Mark is this: "A man will leave his father and mother and be united to his wife, and the two will become one flesh. So they are no longer two, but one. Therefore what God has joined together, let man not separate" (Mk 10:7-8).

The old King James word *cleave* is often associated with this passage. The Hebrew word for "cleave" connotes something akin to Superglue. Remember the advertisement in which two pieces of wood are glued together, and then someone tries to pull them apart? The weaker piece of wood gets shredded, but the glue bond holds.

Divorce works the same way: People's lives get shredded, and the fact of that initial bonding in marriage never goes away completely. It remains a part of a person's identity for life. That is why God hates divorce—because people get hurt.

The second principle of marriage is sanctuary. Take a look at Genesis 2 for a picture of what this principle means. Before God kicked Adam and Eve out of the Garden, he gave them clothing made of animal skins. He recognized their need for protection. Marriage is a form of protection—it is supposed to be the one relationship in the world in which each partner can truly relax and be himself or herself. Husbands and wives should not expose one another to the pain and guilt that comes from lying, pretending and sneaking about.

When alcoholism invades a marriage, sanctuary is an immediate victim. Alcohol builds a wall between spouses that produces as much tension and anguish on both sides as any demilitarized zone. Alcoholics dare not admit the extent of their drinking, yet they grow desperate to stop. Spouses find the very idea of confrontation so ugly and painful that they take the path of least resistance, all the while despairing over their mates' deteriorating mental and physical health. And the children know something is terribly wrong, even though the cover-up conspiracy is in effect around the clock. The impasse appears to be total.

Imagine waking up every morning to an elephant in the middle of the living room. In the alcoholic's home, every member of the family will tiptoe around the elephant. No one takes the initiative to clean up after him or escort him out of the house. Yet everyone complains about the various inconveniences he creates.

The technical term for what happens in a marriage marred by alcoholism is "denial." It is a psychological defense used, without conscious awareness, by both the alcoholic and the spouse to make a grim reality seem more manageable. Christine, in her session with Dave, exhibits denial by saying her husband *cannot* be an alcoholic. What she means is that she cannot bring herself to believe that something as alien as alcoholism is affecting her life and threatening her marriage. Getting past denial and confronting alcoholism head-on is essential for both the alcoholic and the spouse before treatment can begin.

Alcoholism may be an intolerable burden to your marriage. Yet your circumstances are by no means hopeless. Time and time again, people who appeared to be thoroughly enslaved by alcohol have been freed through treatment and long-term follow-up.

We have good news for spouses such as Christine. With some resolve on their part and with assistance from treatment professionals and others who care about the alcoholic (and know about the drinking), bondage to the bottle can be severed. One cannot and must not be expected to try to do it alone. It requires a careful strategy, which we outline in detail in chapter five.

One of the best-known alcoholics of recent years is former First Lady Betty Ford. In her book about recovery from alcoholism and drug addiction, she writes:

When you're suffering from alcoholism, or any other drug dependency, your self-esteem gets so low you're sure nobody would want to bother with you. I think intervention works because suddenly you realize somebody is willing to bother, somebody cares.[2]

Betty Ford is fortunate to have a caring family. And so are we. No matter how bad life became in our marriage—and it

became much worse than that first confrontation at 1 A.M.—
Elsie never stopped caring. Only God knows why.

When we walked down the aisle together in 1966, marriage seemed like stepping into an elevator with the expectation that it would only ascend—going up and up . . . getting
better and better. Instead, to our shock and horror, before we
could push a single button, make a single plan together, all
the cables and pulleys undergirding the elevator came
undone. It began plunging ever faster, carrying us along . . .
powerless to stop it.

Eventually, we did hit bottom, with a crash that will echo
in our memories all our days. Yet we were very fortunate,
very blessed. Through the sustained prayers and guidance of
loved ones and friends, we escaped, became healed and
eventually rejoined one another on a marriage journey that
keeps on improving with time. It is our sincere wish and
prayer that every husband and wife in a marriage being
sabotaged by alcohol would recognize the problem, name it
and find the courage, inspiration and outside help they
require to begin recovering from alcoholism. Our story, and
the counseling advice gleaned from two decades of marriage
and ministry, are meant to help show the way.

To begin, come with us to a mid-sixties Fourth of July
party in Sewickley, Pennsylvania. Dave has just set eyes on
Elsie and made up his mind to get to know her. He's
instantly aware that he must not let on about how much he
drinks. . . .

CHAPTER 2

Hurtling toward Bottom

*E*lsie arrived late to the Fourth of July party. In fact she didn't really want to be there at all. I was there because my parents had just moved to Sewickley, a suburb of Pittsburgh. They were interested in getting to know some of our neighbors, and I was interested in getting to know some single women.

It was 1965, I was twenty-three, and I was looking ahead to my senior year at Yale after having taken three years off from college to serve in the Marine Corps. Elsie had another year of nursing school ahead of her. I didn't know it at the time, but she belonged to a socially prominent family, the Olivers. They are something of a Pittsburgh institution. Four Oliver brothers came there from Ireland in the 1800s and began working in banking and steel. They succeeded handsomely.

Yet Elsie was no snob. As soon as I saw her, I started devising strategies to get acquainted. Now, the ordinary route would be to walk over and introduce myself. Instead, I displayed some of the personality traits that alcoholics tend to have in common: I was devious and manipulative. I didn't want to run the risk of rejection. So I began playing up to Elsie's older sister—checking all the while to see if Elsie was watching. Lo and behold, it worked! The Olivers had a pool party scheduled for the following weekend, and they invited me to come. We began dating after that, and I took great care not to drink excessively when Elsie was around. To put it bluntly, I didn't like myself because of my drinking, and I was sure Elsie wouldn't like me either if she found out.

Like most alcoholics, I cannot identify one particular moment in time when I realized I had a problem with alcohol. It crept up on me gradually, beginning with my drinking habits in high school. We lived in Washington, D.C. My dad was in the navy, and I attended a private school where many parents from Washington's diplomatic community enrolled their children. Frequently, we went to embassy parties where there was plenty of free-flowing booze. One evening, my friends and I visited three of these parties, and I drank a total of seventeen screwdrivers (vodka and orange juice). I remember feeling as if I were walking on air, but I was by no means incapacitated. For a fifteen-year-old boy that is an unusually high level of tolerance for liquor, one of the worrisome signs of potential addiction.

In college I kept on drinking because I liked what it did for me. I tended to be shy, but after a few beers, I would loosen up, start to participate and be one of the guys. That is another sign of potential alcoholism: a personality change caused by drinking. Nonalcoholics may experience a personality change too when they drink, or they may have a different experience. After one or two drinks, they may feel drowsy and uncoordinated. Drinking does not hold an ever-increasing appeal for them as it did for me.

It wasn't long before I was invited to try out for the Tang Cup Team, a Yale parody of its athletic Tyng Cup Team. Each member of the ten-man Tang Cup Team drank two eight-ounce glasses of beer in a carefully orchestrated relay race. My average time per glass was seven-tenths of one second. (And the university supplied our beer.)

My grades deteriorated during my sophomore year to the point where I dropped out of college and joined the Marine Corps for three years. In the service I found plenty of hard-drinking companions. And, while I was stationed in San Diego, I spent more than my share of time on forced overnights in the drunk tank.

In 1965 when I met Elsie, I believed my drinking was still under control even though it was frequent and very heavy. My drink of choice continued to be beer. Elsie didn't suspect that I had a problem with alcohol, even though other people suggested she should be wary. I may have been new in town, but I was gaining a reputation already. Elsie will tell the story of our early courtship from her point of view.

Toward a Perfect Wedding

The last thing I wanted to do on the Fourth of July was to go to a party with my family, so I came dragging in late. And there was Dave. I was immediately impressed by his appearance. He was tall and I liked his smile. As I watched him flirt with my sister, I can remember thinking, "He seems like a very genuine person; he seems so kind." I truly fell in love with him over the next several weeks. We were together almost constantly until the end of the summer, and I just knew he was the one for me. I immediately severed another dating relationship and concentrated all my attention on Dave.

When fall came, Dave went back to college and I started my last year of nursing school in Pittsburgh. One weekend, I drove up to New Haven to see him. As soon as I arrived, we headed for a fraternity party. Dave seemed to know everyone there. He made a beeline for the bar, and came back with drinks for both of us. Before I had sipped half my drink, he had returned to the bar again and again.

I began feeling sleepy, and I marveled at how energetic Dave seemed. He was having a fabulous time. Because it was getting so late, I finally left him there. He stayed and kept on drinking. I dismissed it, thinking, "Well, this is what guys do at college." I had no concept of alcoholism or problem drinking. I did not know how to recognize it, how to respond to a heavy drinker or how to be alert for signs of trouble ahead.

Dave proposed one day when we were both back in Sewickley for the weekend. All he said was, "Let's get married." It seemed so natural; it wasn't even posed as a question. I had no hesitation at all. My response was, "OK, that's a great idea." Mom was really excited, but I was uncertain about how my father would react to the news. Sure enough, after he learned we were serious about getting married, he took me aside.

"Elsie, Dave seems to have some problems with his drinking," Dad said, getting right to the point. "Don't you think the wedding should wait?" I knew in my heart that my Dad was speaking the truth, but I was certain "the problem" would go away.

My family belonged to St. Stephen's Episcopal Church in Sewickley. Later it would become well known for the evangelistic ministry of John Guest, but at the time, it was simply known as a "proper" northeastern Episcopal church. It was the religious hub of society-conscious Sewickley and rather set in its ways.

I had dutifully attended church throughout my childhood, viewing it as an extension of school. After I was confirmed at age thirteen, I considered myself to have graduated from church. I didn't bother going back very often, and I certainly knew nothing about cultivating a personal walk with God.

So at the time I considered the wedding ninety-nine per cent social occasion and maybe one per cent "religious." We received no organized premarital counseling apart from an informal, forty-five-minute chat with the rector. In any event I was not thinking beyond the wedding.

It was a wonderful wedding. There were more than 400 guests present for the evening ceremony on September 10, 1966. Afterwards, there was dinner and dancing at the Allegheny Country Club, which adjoins my parent's property. It was perfect . . . a dream come true, with lovely weather, a lovely dress and plenty of old friends from school. I gave Dave a terrific Omega watch as a wedding present.

We had told everyone we were going to Bermuda for our honeymoon. But my doctor had discovered some tumors on my ovaries. He advised surgery as soon as possible. So we postponed the wedding trip and drove to Michigan City the day after the wedding.

Then came that nightmarish evening at home, waiting for Dave to return from drinking with his softball buddies. Emotionally, I came crashing down from my wedding high and confronted a completely unanticipated aspect of marriage. I had done no reading about marriage, had talked with no one about it, and had no idea how to approach conflict in an intimate relationship.

The following weekend, I returned to Sewickley for my surgery. It was a relief to be home. I didn't have to worry about Dave's behavior: his drinking, his lack of consideration. And I didn't have to feel afraid, at least for a while. The surgery determined that the tumors were benign, but all of one ovary and a large portion of the second had to be removed. The doctors told me I could probably never bear children.

Dave came to visit me on the weekends as I recuperated in the hospital and at my parents' home. After the third weekend he took me back home to Michigan City. At that point, Dave's persistent binge drinking came right out into the open. I had no idea how to cope with it, so I ignored it as best I could. Or I drank along with him. I had little idea at the time how lost he felt, as he will now tell you.

Building a Relationship—with Alcohol
If Elsie lacked a road map for married life, then by comparison I had not even emerged from the wilderness. I lacked any sense of purpose or direction for our life together. There is one aspect of our early dating relationship that helps explain why we—and so many young couples today—are

poorly equipped to enter into a sustained marriage commitment or handle trials such as alcoholism.

By the time Elsie and I went out on a second date after the pool party in mid-July, we were sleeping together. It's not something I am comfortable admitting even now. Partly, it was our enthusiastic "yes" to the spirit of the "do-your-own-thing" 1960s. Partly, I believe, it was a symptom of my own difficulties coping as the adult child of an alcoholic. I had been deprived of warmth and affection from my mother, who drank heavily until she died in 1988. So I sought female affirmation and "love" in bed. That became the goal and purpose of all my dating relationships through college and my Marine Corps days.

What happens when a sexual relationship is put in a position of primary importance? Communication breaks down. Any sort of potentially unacceptable communication is withheld, lest it block the path to the bedroom. So the dating partners do not concentrate on revealing their thoughts and feelings to one another. Instead, the emphasis is on impressing him, or sweeping her off her feet, or otherwise appealing to expectations or to the physical desires of the partner.

In relationships where communication is blocked, an essential ingredient of a successful marriage gets left out. Poor communication virtually ensures that the marriage partners will not "become one" or "cleave" as described in chapter one. And it means the partners will fail to find sanctuary in the marriage. Role-playing can't end at the doorstep, because there is too much at stake. "If she knew what I was *really* like, she'd never stay married to me." That is the message, conscious or subconscious, that plays over and over in the mind of the spouse who feels he has to mask the inner self.

A total lack of communication explains why our first evening in Michigan City turned into such a disaster, why it set a pattern that persisted until the relationship exploded in divorce in 1970.

When I came home from the tavern that evening, I truly thought Elsie was being totally unreasonable; I didn't understand what she was feeling. All that concerned me were my own feelings. I watched her reaction with the same quizzical detachment with which I might have viewed a soap opera. I wondered to myself, "What's the big deal? What's your problem?" For me, drinking and staying out late was normal; for her it was abnormal. And my only expectation for marriage was to have a relationship that was fulfilling.

If a relationship failed to satisfy me, or threatened to get too close to the real me inside, I knew alcohol was always there for an escape. My appetite for liquor never diminished; it just kept growing more intense, more insatiable. Eventually I began going to different liquor stores so no one would catch on that I had a problem. Before long, I was drinking three or four full-sized bottles (known as "fifths") of liquor every week. At one sitting, I would drink an entire bottle. That's how much alcohol it took for me to get drunk. Elsie did not know exactly what to think, but she knew something was dreadfully wrong. She will explain what she saw happening.

Rage and Sympathy
On a typical evening, Dave would come home from work, eat dinner, then get out a bottle. He'd settle down in front of the

television and drink. As time went on, he would binge for two or three days, usually over a weekend. Then he'd stay sober during the work week.

When he was out drinking on the weekends, I constantly worried about him. One evening, a police officer telephoned in the middle of the night. "Mrs. MacKenzie? Your husband has been arrested for drunk driving. You can come down to the station and get him out tomorrow. No use coming tonight; he's out cold."

The next morning, humiliated, I crept into the station. I couldn't even look as a policeman shook Dave out of his stupor and released him. When we got home, I helped Dave get into the house and into bed. I happened to look at one of his wrists, then the other. "Dave," I said, "Where's your watch?" It was no use; he had passed out again. The Omega watch—my wedding gift to him—was gone. He has no idea how he lost it. We presume a cellmate relieved him of it while he slept in jail.

Finally, I began to read about alcoholism. I latched onto Marty Mann's *Primer on Alcoholism,* a classic in the field by a woman member of AA. In it she describes some of the early signs of alcoholism. As I read, it seemed as if the author kept referring specifically to Dave. Alcoholism may be strongly suspected, she wrote, when someone:

1. Makes promises about drinking—saying, "I know my limit now; I'll have to be more careful next time."
2. Minimizes the number of drinks he had at any one time.
3. Gulps his drinks.
4. Takes a drink before going to a party where there will be more drinking.

5. Feels it is necessary to have drinks at certain regular times—cocktails before lunch; drinks at 5:30.

6. Must have drinks with any special event.

7. Must have drinks to combat fatigue, nerves, worries, depression.[1]

The book points out that these behavioral symptoms:

indicate a compulsion to drink rather than to see the situation through by other means. Often enough the incipient alcoholic recognizes that drinking is out of order at that particular time or place, but does not seem able to control his urge to have drinks. Often, too, he recognizes and even agrees verbally that one or two drinks should be plenty under the circumstances, but he seems driven to make it three, four, or five, regardless of his statements, and regardless of the conspicuous position it may put him in.[2]

Mann's book also describes ways in which a wife might respond to an alcoholic husband. There is a peculiar tendency for spouses of alcoholics (and particularly wives) to go to two very different extremes as they try to cope. I was no exception. In anger and frustration about Dave's drinking, I would explode with accusations and demands. Other times, my nursing instincts would surface and all I wanted to do was protect him and make him well. That was true particularly when the alcohol began eating away at his stomach, causing gastritis. He was confined to a hospital bed for a while one time, needing to rest and change his diet. And I became Nurse Fuzzy Wuzzy, making it all better.

Later in this book, you will learn how an alcoholic feels and why he or she cannot begin to improve until alcohol is refused permanently and completely. Most spouses labor under the assumption that they can make their alcoholic behave better by the way they act. It just isn't so. In our case no matter what I did, Dave's dependency on alcohol only kept increasing. And his behavior grew more and more alarming.

One day, after I'd learned I was pregnant (against all odds), Dave got out his M-1 rifle and paced through the house with it. "I just don't see any hope," he muttered. "I'm going to do it. I'm going to get it over with." I tried to breathe steadily and keep my hand from shaking as I called the police. "Come over here right away," I told them. "My husband has a gun."

Dave heard me make the call, so he sat down at the kitchen table and began taking the gun apart. When the police arrived, they were afraid to come to the door. I saw two officers out front, keeping their distance. I opened the front door and waved them in. By this time, Dave was asleep— passed out at the kitchen table. I put the pieces of the gun in a bag and handed it to one of the officers. He told me, "I can't keep this, Ma'am, since no one got hurt, and the gun wasn't even fired. You'll have to come and get it at the station tomorrow."

The next day, we drove to the station together to pick up the gun. Dave put on his usual, affable front for the police. "My wife must have been hallucinating," he joked. "I was only cleaning my gun."

At a low point such as this, a spouse may feel it's the "last straw." A direct confrontation with the alcoholic has been avoided for months and perhaps years, but something has changed: the relationship appears to have reached a point of no return. Being pregnant, I grew deeply concerned about my child's safety in a home with a drunken, gun-toting father.

With no professional assistance and no knowledge about intervening in the life of an alcoholic, I confronted him. I didn't harp on the drinking itself. Instead, it was our marriage I was concerned about.

"Dave, we don't have a marriage," I said icily. "This is just no good. Something's got to give." Dave sat brooding on the sofa. I could tell he was miserable, yet he would never talk about it, never let on that the drinking had taken possession of him. I didn't get any response at all, really, until our son Hector was born three days before Christmas in 1967.

Dave came into my hospital room after Hector was born and sat down next to my bed. He brought in a little tree, decorated with blinking lights. "I'm going to give up drinking," he said softly, "because I am so thrilled about our son." It felt wonderful to hear him say that.

"My whole life is going to be different now," I thought. "Everything really *is* going to be all right."

The following March, we moved to a ten-acre fruit tree farm in Baroda, Michigan, and Dave landed a job with Heathkit Company, a manufacturer of do-it-yourself kits for electronic items. We knew nothing whatsoever about farming. Yet for Dave it was a dream come true. He had spent all his summers as a young boy visiting his grandmother and grandfather on their ranch in California, where they grew oranges. Because of Dave's warm memories of his time in California, he had always wanted to live on a farm.

As we planned our move to Michigan, everything seemed perfect. We had a beautiful baby boy, Dave had a new job and he had vowed to quit drinking. He will explain how quickly the dream shattered.

A Rough Landing

Eventually I learned that I had tried to stop drinking for all the wrong reasons: to make Elsie happy (and get her off my back) and for my new baby son. And I believed making a clean break with the past by moving and starting a new job would mean I could do without alcohol. I did not grasp the need to change my life for *my* sake. I tried to do it on my own, using willpower, without any outside treatment or support. Any recovering alcoholic will tell you that this is a recipe for certain failure. During those six months "on the wagon," I became progressively grouchier and harder to live with. My resolve to stay dry was wearing thin because my marriage didn't seem to be improving anyway. It wasn't long at all before I began looking for an excuse to have a drink.

That excuse came after some friends helped us move to the farm. After the work was done, someone suggested we relax with a few beers. I jumped at the chance to go to the store and buy several six-packs. And it wouldn't be polite to let them drink on their own. I popped into the kitchen of our farmhouse on my way out and said, "Elsie, the guys and I are going to have a couple of quick beers together." She said nothing, and I was hurrying out the door. Out of the corner of my eye, I could see her face fall. For me, that old familiar mix of insecurity and living on the edge of failure flooded back, but I managed to suppress it as I dashed headlong for the liquor store.

By saying I was going to have "just a few" beers, I was able to fool myself, if not Elsie. Having "just a few" is rarely a realistic possibility for an alcoholic. For me, having "just a few" triggered my body's craving for more and more and more. I don't recall what happened when I came home that evening . . . if I came home that evening.

That single departure from my vow to stop drinking made me feel as if I were being released from a six-month prison term. The old alcohol-induced euphoria returned. My Christmastime vow to Elsie meant nothing to me, and alcohol again took control.

Evenings, particularly on the weekends, were prime time for drinking bouts away from home that lasted until 4 or 5 A.M. One evening, a police officer pulled me over as my car weaved toward home. I failed a sobriety test miserably and was placed under arrest. The penalty was a suspended driver's license for thirty days.

During that time Elsie drove me to work every morning and picked me up every afternoon. Since she had more control that month over my coming and going, she arranged for us to visit a psychiatrist. With no training whatsoever about alcoholism, that psychiatrist told me exactly what I wanted to hear.

At one point I mustered the courage to admit the truth: "I believe I have a drinking problem." He completely dismissed my admission. "No," he said. "You have pressures at home and pressures at work. We'll deal with those and then your drinking will return to normal." He prescribed Librium, a tranquilizer.

I generated what I thought was a convincing bravado about the shape my life was in, but inwardly guilt and fear were exacting a severe toll. Elsie may not have realized it at the time, but another passage in the Marty Mann book she was reading paints an eerily accurate portrait of my state of mind:

The fact that his drinking is different from other people's

is constantly showing up, with a consequent increase in
his bewilderment and fear. Unless he has learned something about alcoholism and its progressive symptoms . . .
he cannot understand what is happening to him. . . . He
is making superhuman efforts to hold it in check. His
repeated failures terrify him, and make him doubt his
sanity. But if he is insane, he should be locked up, he
thinks, . . . and this he cannot face. So he is forced to deny
the whole frightening picture, to try to explain it away, to
put it in terms he can understand. He is fighting for his
belief in his own sanity, without which he cannot function.[3]

In January 1970 our marriage began its final descent toward
the "bottom" which we both believed we had hit many times
before. Our second son, Davie, was born. This time, I made
no promises to stop drinking, no contrite visits to Elsie's
hospital room.

Two months later, I could barely face Elsie. I could not
come to grips with being a father (and a failure at it) for the
second time, so I told Elsie I had to go away for a while. "I'm
going to a motel for the weekend," I said vaguely. "I really
need to get away and sort things out."

Without a word of further discussion, I took off for
Washington, D.C., intent on seeing an old girlfriend there. As
I drove, I tossed down can after can of beer, just as I had on
our post-wedding trip to Indiana. My drinking so alarmed a
hitchhiker I picked up that he wanted out after less than one
hundred miles. When I telephoned Elsie a day and a half
after I left, she was frantic. And, for the first time, she was
willing to take action. Before I could do any explaining, she
told me, "Dave, I'm leaving. My parents are here; the boys

and I are going back to Sewickley with them."

The cracks in my facade were widening so swiftly that there was no concealing my despair any longer. In a desperate bid for help, recognition, sympathy—any response, really—I said, "Elsie, I'm going to kill myself. Bury me next to my grandfather in California." For once, she stood fast. "Don't be ridiculous, Dave. Get back here and go see the psychiatrist."

I was hurt, but I knew I deserved nothing less. She was miserable and I had made her that way. I felt helpless and desperate and terribly angry. I created a ruckus in two D.C. bars and got thrown out of both. It was an ugly spectacle, yet it was the first time I began to come to grips with my personal responsibility. Not that I was willing to do something to change; instead, I found myself relying even more heavily on alcohol to numb the emotional pain.

After several days, I drove back to the Michigan farmhouse. Without Elsie and the boys there, it seemed as barren and forbidding as the Badlands. I telephoned my boss and quit my job on the spot.

I did go back to the psychiatrist, who dutifully kept refilling my prescriptions for Librium and sleeping pills. My suicide threat on the phone to Elsie was a bluff, but the realities of my messed-up life made suicide appear to be my only escape. I began hoarding my prescription pills. One day, in a black depression, I called the psychiatrist. I wanted someone to get the message.

"Come out to the house," I told him. "I don't see any way out of this mess. I need some advice." When he arrived, I took him to the dining room. There, on the table, I had on display every possible implement for taking my own life: my M-1 rifle, a butcher knife, a rope. The only things missing were the bottles of pills I'd been stashing away.

At that point, my bravado returned and I made the situation appear to be a joke. "Which method is the best?" I asked him. "I don't want it to be too painful." He didn't take me seriously. "Get some rest, Dave," he told me. "Get out and see some people, look for another job."

Like so many alcoholics, I sank deeper into isolation and depression. I thought I knew what I wanted from life. I wanted to be happy and productive, to be respected by friends and loved by my family. I was achieving none of it. My twisted cries for help hadn't worked: no one cared that I wanted to kill myself. I was running out of money, Elsie would not think of coming back, even though I begged her to several times on the phone, and I was certain I could not make it through a job interview. Everything was closing in on me. I was suffocating beneath a blanket of self-imposed misery, and I saw no escape.

One afternoon I sat down at the kitchen table with none of the garish implements I had displayed earlier. All I had in front of me was an eight-ounce glass of water and two bottles of pills. I wrote no note, placed no last-second telephone calls.

I began swallowing the pills as quickly as I could and chased them with the water. Just like the old Tang Cup Team, I mused. It didn't even take a second.

Three days later, I woke up in a hospital bed with my parents there. A teenager from the next farm had come to the house, walked up on the porch and peered through the window. He saw me crumpled on the kitchen floor and called a rescue squad. I have no idea why he came, or when.

The day after I woke up, my father and mother drove me home to Sewickley. They never said a word about the incident, or about my drinking. Once again, they tiptoed around the elephant in our living room. An open discussion of the problem and possible solutions never occurred. Denial held fast, but only for a week or so.

CHAPTER 3

What a Spouse Endures

*T*hree weeks elapsed between the time Elsie returned home to Sewickley with her parents and when Dave attempted suicide. Exhausted and aching inside, Elsie slept thirteen hours straight on her first night back home. For several days her parents watched their two grandsons, Hector and Davie, while Elsie began sorting out what had happened.

Elsie retreated to the comfort of her old bedroom. Lying on the bed, she gazed at the familiar curtains catching the breeze and at a bookcase full of memorabilia from school. She could scarcely believe she had endured such a nightmarish marriage. In the safety of her parents' home Elsie felt as if she could will away the memories and restore her life magically to its pre-Dave MacKenzie days.

But then the telephone would ring. "Elsie?" her dad would say. "It's for you." Particularly if it was late in the day, Elsie knew it was Dave. Their conversations were as predictable as the minutes in an hour: "Elsie? How are the boys doing? I really want to see them. Please bring them back home."

She trotted out the same reply each time, like a recording. "No, Dave. We are staying here. It's over. I am not coming back."

One evening, after several weeks had passed, the telephone rang and Elsie tensed up. Here we go again, she thought. Her dad answered the phone and carried on a very terse conversation; he didn't summon Elsie to the phone. As soon as he hung up, she could tell something serious had happened. Her dad asked her to sit down in the living room.

"Elsie," he said, "that was Dave's father. Dave tried to kill himself today, and he almost succeeded. He's in the hospital now, and his parents are on their way to pick him up."

Elsie was surprised at how calm she felt. "So," she thought, "he really tried to kill himself after all the empty threats." She had detached herself so completely from Dave and the very idea of being married to him that it seemed as if her dad was speaking about someone else . . . certainly not her husband.

Alcoholism may claim only one marriage partner, but inevitably it victimizes both. And it does not stop there. Numerous people—even whole families and extended families—may find themselves struggling with the devastation brought on by one alcoholic. As we have already mentioned, the spouse of the alcoholic generally bears the brunt of the disease.

What goes on in the mind and heart of a person coping

with an alcoholic spouse? Could their actions or behavior somehow *cause* alcoholism? Is it worth trying to salvage a marriage when a drinking spouse refuses to quit ... refuses even to acknowledge there is a problem? Elsie picks up our story in this chapter and takes you deep within the hidden interior of a dying marriage.

Choosing Divorce

My parents and I knew exactly when Dave returned to Sewickley with his parents. In a small town everyone knows everything just as soon as it happens. Because of his persistent telephone calls before the suicide attempt, we worried about being harassed further. We called the police and told them, "If you see a 1966 hunter-green Mustang with Michigan plates, tell the driver he's not welcome anywhere around our house." I couldn't bear to look at the car—much less the driver—now that our marriage was a wreck.

Dave did leave us alone, and emotionally I let go of him and the marriage as the days passed. It was summertime, and I was preoccupied with the boys. In the mornings we'd fill a wading pool in the yard and splash and play. Then, while the boys napped, I would talk with old friends and weigh my options. The cold reality of obtaining a divorce hadn't actually occurred to me, yet I felt myself being steered decisively in that direction.

My parents maintained a hands-off approach. They were wonderful; they never said "I told you so"; never tapped me on the shoulder with a reminder of what they'd said about Dave's drinking. Yet other relatives and friends were brimming with advice.

"So, what are your plans, Elsie?" I got so tired of that

question! I didn't have any plans . . . didn't want any plans. I just craved a season of taking life one day at a time. "You can't go back to him," my friends would say with conviction. "Think about it—he's not going to change. Nothing you've tried has worked so far. He's just not cut out to be a decent husband."

As I spoke with family and friends that summer, I discovered how abnormal my marriage experience was. All along, I had fooled myself over and over into thinking our relationship was routine and that we simply had some adjustments to make after the wedding. I learned that it is not routine for a wife to wait up wondering when a husband is coming home, night after night. It is not routine to telephone one bar after another from the Yellow Pages, checking up on a missing spouse. It is not routine to deny the obvious so skillfully for so long. My parents never pressured me to get a divorce. Yet, particularly after his suicide attempt, I felt a compelling need to make a clean break from Dave, to formalize the complete emotional separation I felt from him. Before that first summer ended, I traveled back to Michigan to file divorce papers. I would not consider waiting the one year required by the state of Pennsylvania.

When the judge handed me the final divorce papers after my court appearance, I felt thoroughly empty, drained and sad. I was twenty-seven years old, and my marriage was ruined.

Then my aunt, Betsy Drain, sat me down for a talk. She had married an alcoholic years before, and they were divorced. She told me, "Elsie, you're divorced and you're hurting. Don't make any major decisions in your life for two years. Stay where you are, don't move, don't do anything rash." For some reason, I listened to her. Her calm, steady spirit was exactly what I needed in the midst of all the turmoil.

I have never forgotten my aunt's wise words, and I frequently give the same advice to women who walk out on alcoholic husbands. Unless there is a compelling reason to do otherwise, they should wait before they file for divorce— wait, in fact, before making any permanent, life-changing decisions. In most cases, women who are coping with an alcoholic husband are so wounded inside that they can no longer think clearly. Many are similar to Christine, whose circumstances were outlined in chapter one. They have little or no knowledge about alcoholism. They do not grasp how deeply it is affecting not only the addicted spouse but the entire family.

Held Hostage

An alcoholic home is a household under siege. Husband and wife and children all are captives. One alcoholic treatment specialist refers to family members as "alcohostages." Clinical psychologist Morris Kokin, in *Women Married to Alcoholics,* explains what happens to the spouse:

The alcohostage, like the hostage, feels an overwhelming sense of helplessness and powerlessness. No matter what she does or tries, she soon discovers that she has no control over the alcoholic's drinking. She experiences shame and humiliation as a result both of the drinking itself and of her inability to control it. As happens to other hostages, her self-worth, self-esteem, and confidence are deeply shaken. The alcohostage is left feeling confused and bewildered, unable to comprehend fully what is happening around her and to her and what to do about it.[1]

Spouses of alcoholics tend to share these traits in common, yet their efforts to change their circumstances vary greatly. Some hostages plot their escape while others become passive and dependent upon their captors. My responses to Dave's drinking ran the gamut, from ignoring the problem to participating in his drinking to separation and divorce.

Until I began to understand alcoholism, nothing worked. And by then, we were separated. Dave's eventual decision to stop drinking, join AA, and remain sober was his own, not the result of any pressuring or cajoling on my part.

Believe me, I had done my share of badgering. It didn't work. Dave's drinking habits did not change. When one marriage partner desperately wants to see change, and the other partner cannot change, the stage is set for extremely high levels of frustration.

For me, frustration usually erupted into rage at a point of total exhaustion. After waiting up for Dave, or being awakened in the middle of the night when he came home, I would explode in anger. "Dave, look what this is doing to you! You just can't keep on drinking so much. It's ruining our marriage." This sort of "home remedy," as author Marty Mann calls it, is an abysmal failure.

Placing blame, pointing fingers and shouting at an alcoholic generates a like reaction. Dave verbally attacked me (unjustly) after that first post-wedding "night on the town" because I had attacked him (justly) for failing to come home when he said he would. To say the least, my screeching and throwing things did not even begin to move Dave in the direction of treatment and recovery. It only antagonized him and drove him to say things that were not true but hurt me deeply.

"Who wouldn't drink if they were married to you?" That is a favorite defense of alcoholics, claiming the spouse (or children or boss) "drive them to drink." Often, when the alcoholic tries to project blame onto other people, those being blamed do not know what to think. In the upside-down world of an alcoholic marriage a spouse may respond by feeling guilty. The thought that there was something wrong with me kept gnawing at me during the early weeks and months of our marriage, and Dave reinforced that self-doubt at every turn, whenever the subject of his drinking came up.

My diminishing self-esteem was one reason I felt I could not tell anyone about the problem. I never dared to ask for help, seek advice or confide even in my parents. Partly, I wanted to "save face" and keep up an appearance of happiness and success. Because I had no concept of alcoholism as a disease, I was deeply ashamed of Dave's behavior. How could it fail but to reflect poorly on me?

To the world outside our marriage I concealed the truth as skillfully and as long as I could. This same way of coping often occurs among spouses of alcoholics. They start avoiding social occasions where the alcoholic spouse might cause a scene. They routinely make excuses to the husband's boss about why he is late (or absent) when the workday begins.

By telephoning the office on a hung-over Monday morning and by turning down social invitations, the nonalcoholic spouse prevents the alcoholic from facing the consequences of his drinking. Unwittingly, these spouses make it possible—even likely—that the alcoholic will keep on doing the very thing that is ripping apart the marriage. Often, these dutiful spouses are said to "enable" the drinking, but that should not be taken as a put-down. The wives who are "enablers" believe they are doing the right thing. They see their actions as reasonable, loyal and correct, given their circumstances. Besides, as in the case of telephoning the boss, they are usually doing exactly what their husbands asked them to do!

Putting on a happy face for the outside world to see may make it easier for the wife to continue in the most insidious lie of all: the lie to herself. In the comic strip *Peanuts,* a familiar ritual plays itself out each autumn. As surely as the leaves begin to fall, Lucy snatches a football away from Charlie Brown just as he revs up to kick it. Each time, Charlie Brown fools himself into thinking, "It won't happen again." Then he falls flat on his back. Similarly, the spouse of an alcoholic keeps on believing "it will be different this time." When it isn't different, the spouse is once again knocked flat emotionally.

As alcoholism progresses to its later stages, a steady shift in responsibility occurs in the marriage. Eventually, the wife takes charge of virtually everything: paying the bills, keeping the house and yard up, spending time with the children and taking care (as best she can) of their needs. Loneliness and uncertainty become constant companions, even at the oddest times.

Habits and behaviors such as these are typical of what is known as "codependency." In response to Dave's alcoholism, I adjusted my entire life and my whole world view to accommodate his addiction. Codependency is an unhealthy way of controlling interior feelings by attempting to exert control over others and their behavior. As I learned, codependency requires a healing process. There are no easy routes of escape.

Once, as Dave's drinking became damagingly heavy, we took a vacation. We drove to the Black Hills of South Dakota to see Mount Rushmore and spend a few days "away from it all." I should have known better. "It all" came right along with us. No sooner were we settled into our motel room than Dave disappeared without a word. He stayed out most of the night, barhopping. And there I was, hand-wringing and fretting as always when I was supposed to be relaxing and having fun.

Sex and Alcoholism

It almost goes without saying that an intimate, physical relationship with an alcoholic spouse is often abandoned altogether. If not, it becomes a matter of grudging endurance on the part of the nonalcoholic. Also, the reality of extramarital affairs looms large in alcoholic homes. Denial takes hold in this part of the relationship as well, and it burdens both spouses with even more suppressed emotional turmoil.

The basis for a satisfying sex life in marriage is mutual trust and respect. In the marriage taken hostage by alcohol, those factors are undermined by fear and revulsion. In many cases actual physical and sexual abuse occur. Even when they do not (as in our case), sustained fear takes a heavy toll. I feared Dave's drunken driving, beginning just one day after our wedding reception. I feared for his ability to continue working and for his safety at all hours of the night, in all sorts of disreputable places. I feared for myself and most of all for our two little boys.

In chapter one, Dave wrote about the importance of unity

in marriage, as well as the concept of sanctuary, or mutual protection—a sense of shared safety and comfort. Even if a marriage is anchored by these principles, alcohol cuts it loose from these moorings. Arresting the drift toward certain shipwreck is not easy, and it is not a task to attempt alone. Yet it is possible; there are some tried and true means to combat the terror of alcoholism in marriage.

Setting the Marriage Free

I wish I could say that I knew enough—or cared enough—in 1970 to have confronted Dave successfully with his desperate need for treatment and follow-up through AA. I wish I would have been in contact with professionals adept at addressing alcoholism, rather than a psychiatrist who advised Dave to solve his problems at work instead of focusing on his inability to drink normally.

In our case, Dave hit bottom hard and nearly died. I abandoned him in pure disgust, frustration and anger. Fortunately for us, the events of March 1970 jolted Dave into a sudden, stark awareness of his problem, its all-consuming nature and his personal responsibility to acknowledge and combat it.

Our marriage did not have to explode as it did, and Dave did not have to sink to the depths of despair. Now I know the alternatives, the ways in which others have approached alcoholism as an illness that can be arrested but not cured. For the nonalcoholic spouse, that process begins with some important adjustments in attitude and behavior.

Here are some of the steps I should have taken, steps I now advise wives like Christine to follow:

1. Learn all there is to know about alcoholism. Beginning

with the resource list at the back of this book, find out what doctors, psychologists, recovering alcoholics and their spouses have to say about their experiences with the disease.

2. Attend a number of AA's open meetings. There you will hear alcoholics at all stages of recovery talk about how they feel, what they are going through, what hurts and what helps.

3. Contact your local chapter of Al-Anon, an organization patterned after AA which holds meetings for family members. Even before your alcoholic spouse begins attending AA, you can benefit from the support and camaraderie offered by Al-Anon. There you will discover ways in which other spouses are coping. You will meet plenty of people married to alcoholics. And just about all of them will know what you have been experiencing from day to day. They've been there too.

The chief value of Al-Anon, according to many who have participated in it, is an opportunity to rebuild lost confidence and self-esteem. The meetings focus on the nonalcoholic spouse; discussions about the alcoholic himself are strictly forbidden, so the meetings do not turn into "gripe sessions." Instead, Al-Anon offers a means for spouses to re-enter the mainstream of life, to connect with friends and family from whom they'd withdrawn and to regain a sense that life is worth living—with or without an alcoholic spouse.

4. It's easier said than done, but you need to begin behaving differently toward your alcoholic spouse by exercising what is known as "detachment." Now that you know more about addiction, you know it is nothing to be ashamed of. By displaying a new attitude toward your spouse's drinking, you improve the climate for discussion and recognition of the real

issue: the need for treatment and recovery. Detachment means gaining perspective on the drinking and the drinker; it means setting aside personal feelings of disgust, contempt or impatience and replacing them with compassion, realism and hope.

Marty Mann, in her *New Primer on Alcoholism,* puts it this way:

Up to now the alcoholic has been made to feel shame if he could not handle his drinking by himself. Our goal must be to reverse that: to make him feel shame at not seeking help for his illness. If he himself really comes to believe that he has a disease, the chances are greatly enhanced that he will seek treatment for it.[2]

5. Part of behaving differently means no more cover-ups: no more lies or "enabling" activities such as telephoning the boss on Monday morning. Wives understandably fear that life will get much worse if their husband's drinking comes out into the open. They fear he will lose his job, lose the respect of friends, children and extended family. Yet when they view their lives and their marriages with some detachment, they recognize that "worse" may be necessary before life can eventually get "better." Bringing the alcoholic face to face with the consequences of his drinking is essential.

When that happens—when the boss knows the truth, when his children understand—then the alcoholic may be more likely to agree to begin professional treatment. Until it happens, his fabrications remain safely intact, and there is no incentive to change.

6. Resist the temptation to send silent signals to your alcoholic by throwing away his liquor or monitoring how much he drinks. Let him learn that you will no longer excuse

his behavior or cover his tracks. If you do deliver a threat or an ultimatum, such as "Next time you stay out all night, I'm leaving," be prepared to do so. Separation is extremely difficult, scary and threatening to many women. Consider doing it only if you believe that's what it will take to bring him face to face with the realities of what alcohol is doing to his life.

7. If you choose to stick with the marriage and not leave, even temporarily, select an alcohol treatment specialist to help you plan a strategy of intervention. In many cases, intervention is a way of causing the alcoholic to confront reality long before he would on his own. It can save much grief and pain.

The Road to Reconciliation

For me, help came from a most unlikely source: from the church I believed I had "graduated" from . . . the church where we celebrated such a festive wedding on a day that seemed to have passed by centuries before. The first suggestion about my returning to church came from my dad: "Elsie, there's a new, young minister over at St. Stephen's," my dad told me. "Whoa," I thought. "That's all I need." I dismissed the suggestion without a second thought.

Then on a December day just after our divorce had become final, an old friend named Chip Nix stopped by to see me.

"I understand things have been difficult lately," he said. I was noncommittal, but I told him the divorce was final. "That's all behind me now," I said. I had no idea what was ahead, however, and when I let myself think about it, that was terrifying.

"Let me tell you what's been happening in my life," Chip

said. "I've become a Christian. When Jesus came into my life, it was as if I had been transformed into a completely new person."

I was polite but chilly as I told Chip, "Well, that's great for you." Yet something about Chip was decidedly different. He sat on the edge of his chair, his eyes bright and caring. "How can anyone be so genuinely sure and absolutely overjoyed about something like this?" I remember asking myself.

Before he left, Chip handed me a booklet entitled "The Four Spiritual Laws." He insisted I meet John Guest, that new minister at St. Stephen's. To humor him, I went to meet John and his wife, Kathie, at their home one day.

There was something so warm and comforting about the atmosphere in their home that I lingered until everyone else had left. Kathie was kind, but direct. She asked, "Would you like to talk about anything?" I made no attempt to hide my ignorance about spiritual things, which were clearly so important to Kathie and her friends, so I lamely replied, "I don't know what to ask you." Kathie knew all about the divorce, all about Dave's drinking (who didn't?), yet she never mentioned my circumstances at all. Instead, she began talking about Jesus. I don't remember a word of it now, but I can recall her tone of voice and her genuineness as if it were yesterday. I began going to church services and attending a Bible study.

I put off making a personal commitment to Christ, though by this time I understood what was required of me: I knew I had to respond to what Jesus did for me, and I was convinced it was real. Kathie prodded me one day. "Elsie, aren't you ready to ask Christ into your life now?"

I'd been reading *Mere Christianity* by C. S. Lewis, and the message was beginning to hit home. "Not yet," I told Kathie. "I just have to read one more book." Kathie wouldn't let up. "Elsie, it's as if you are sitting in jail and the door is open. You keep saying 'I'm not going anywhere yet.' "

Kathie's words kept ringing in my ears, so one night when I put the boys to bed, I said a short prayer. "Lord my life is a mess, my marriage is ruined, my life is falling apart. I can't handle it. I don't know what to do. Please take my life and do something with it."

Well, I thought, so much for that. Nothing happened; I didn't feel any different right away. I didn't even mention it to Kathie. Then about a week later, as I was driving, the whole Episcopal morning prayer service came back to me—all the songs and prayers I'd heard since I was young. At once, the significance of it became clear to me. It was more than just a hollow recitation; all those words about God were true! It was as if all the pieces of a puzzle had suddenly come together.

Before and after I made my commitment to Jesus, the women I had been meeting with accepted me for who I was. There was never any hint of judgment, whispering or looking askance at me because I was divorced from an alcoholic husband. Frequently, people at church would ask how long I'd been divorced, but I was never shunned or treated differently. Just the opposite happened in fact.

At one point, Kathie Guest said to me, "Why don't we start a mother's group?" "We?" I said. Kathie replied, "Yes. You have it at your house, and I'll help." So there I was: a divorced woman leading a Bible study on being a wife and mother.

During that study, the idea of reconciling with Dave first

began to germinate. I resisted it and tried to root it out. It happened as we studied a passage in the Bible which says, "A wife must not separate from her husband. But if she does, she must remain unmarried or else be reconciled to her husband" (1 Cor 7:10-11). Those words jumped off the page at me as if they'd been printed in fluorescent ink.

I dug in my heels at once and thought, "I'm not going to do either!" I found it really troubling. "Why did Paul have to say that? That's not fair!" When the divorce was final, I had decided that I was not going to date around. I was not going to fall for anyone on the rebound and find myself being used.

At the same time, I knew I wanted to be married. I desperately wanted a father for Hector and Davie. So I found myself praying along these lines: "Okay Lord, I'm divorced now. Aren't there any Christian guys I can go out with?" A little voice in my head kept saying, "What about your ex-husband?" And I would shout "No, that isn't fair!" I rejected the very idea of it because of my memories of hurt and fear.

Relentlessly, suggestions about reconciliation pursued me. One day I was standing in Kathie's kitchen, helping her do the dishes. Out of the blue, she asked, "Do you think you and Dave will ever get back together again?" Her question bothered me, and I cut her off cold. "No. It's not possible."

Yet I had to admit things were different with Dave. I was aware that he had been attending AA meetings and he was even coming to church at St. Stephen's, although he studiously avoided going to the same service that I attended.

We saw each other weekly when I dropped the boys off at his parents' house so that he could visit with them for half a day. We scarcely said two words to one another apart from arranging pick-up times. It was clear he wasn't drinking: he actually showed up on time to see the boys, and he no longer looked drawn and disheveled. Still, I had no feeling for him whatsoever. Taking the boys to see him felt no different from taking them to an appointment at the pediatrician's.

There was one instance, about six months after I left Dave, when my impression of him shifted just a notch away from pure dislike and distrust. He telephoned my parents, asking if he could stop by their house because he "had something to tell them." Mom agreed and arranged for him to come at 1 P.M. the next day.

She came over to my apartment with a puzzled look on her face. "Dave just called," she said. "He's going to stop by tomorrow." I asked if I could be there too. I didn't want anything going on behind my back.

Mom, Dad and I waited on the patio as 1 P.M. approached. Hector and Davie were indoors napping. We heard the Mustang pull up in the driveway, and he came around back. He was there on time! He wore a dark suit, and his shoes were freshly polished. He was clear-eyed and cleanly shaven.

Dad stood up, shook Dave's hand perfunctorily and invited him to sit down. Dave cleared his throat and stared at the patio floor. He never once looked toward me.

"I am attending AA meetings every night," Dave explained. "They give you a series of steps to work through, and one of the steps is to make amends to people you have hurt." At this point, Dave looked up. "I'd like to ask your forgiveness for the things I've done to your daughter and to you. I know you've been hurt in all this too, and I want to apologize."

That was it. Mom and Dad responded very coolly. "Thank

you for coming," they said. Then Dave left.

I was stunned. One part of me reacted cynically. "Well, it's about time, after all I've been through," I thought. Yet there was no denying that a significant change had come over Dave. I didn't realize it completely at the time, but AA's twelve steps were bringing him face to face with the reality of what he'd done to his life and his marriage. The old manipulative, fast-talking Dave appeared to be gone; he hadn't seemed interested in trying to get me to come back. He told us he was following the AA steps because he needed to in order to recover. I believed him.

I said nothing to my parents, apart from a vague remark about being surprised to see him looking so pulled together. We never discussed it. I went back inside where the boys were sleeping. Gazing at Hector, now a lanky preschooler, I recalled how hopeful I'd felt just after he was born. That was one of several times Dave swore he'd give up drinking. Are things really any different now? I wondered. Will Dave be able to stick with AA? I had no sense of certainty about that, but one thing was clear: Dave was in better emotional and physical shape than I'd ever seen him before.

Was he truly well? Would he stay well? I later learned that Dave had his own hopes and fears about these things. But let him describe them.

CHAPTER 4

What the Alcoholic Endures

*C*oming back home after a failed suicide attempt with no job and no wife was certainly the lowest point of my life. In AA parlance I had "hit bottom." The doctors in Michigan who brought me around by pumping all those pills out of my stomach had put me on Antabuse, a somewhat outdated drug used to treat alcoholism. It makes people violently ill if they drink even a small amount of liquor.

It really didn't matter to me that I couldn't drink; in fact, nothing mattered to me at all. Emotionally, I was like a zombie: drained and numb. My mother arranged for me to have a complete physical, and I can recall going through all sorts of tests and psychotherapy. I kept wishing the doctors would find something wrong with me ... a brain tumor, cancer, anything that might explain why I couldn't cope and couldn't even drink normally. When they pronounced me well, I was deeply disillusioned.

About a month after I arrived in Sewickley, Mom and Dad dragged me to a party. I had no desire to see anyone, say anything or go anywhere, but I went along to humor my parents. At the party, I met John L. (I did not know it when I met him, but John was a member of Alcoholics Anonymous. In keeping with AA's principle of anonymity, his last name will remain confidential.) "Would you like some club soda?" he asked me. "That's what I'm having." I didn't know it at the time, but it was a set-up. John and I were talking in a room away from the crowd, and he told me, "I am an alcoholic, so I stay away from booze."

I didn't intend to respond, but for some reason, the truth popped out. "I believe I have a problem with alcohol too," I told him. There. I said it; it was out in the open. Maybe he would have something more enlightened to tell me than my old friend, the Librium-pushing psychiatrist in Michigan.

John handed me some literature about Alcoholics Anonymous, and he invited me to a meeting at his house the following Thursday evening. I went to the meeting convinced it would not hold any answers for me. Yet there was a level of desperation in me that said, "I've got to do this. I'll go with the program, no matter what it is."

In John's living room there were half-a-dozen men and women sitting in chairs and talking. I pulled up a chair and listened in amazement. Here were ordinary-looking people describing exactly the same sort of behavior and feelings I'd been having ever since my drinking got out of control. They, too, had messed up their lives and their marriages. They were struggling with the physical symptoms that accumulate with sustained drinking. They had lied to their bosses, missed work and angered their families, all because they had to drink. They had battled shame, guilt, loneliness and desperation. And yet, today they were sober, and at least reasonably well-adjusted and happy. They had what I wanted.

At one point, I spoke up and began to tell about how I felt. John broke in right away. "Shut up, Dave," he said. "You're not here to talk, you're here to learn. I'll tell you when it's time for you to talk."

That's exactly what I needed—someone to talk to me straight from the shoulder. It was my first introduction to AA and the first time in a very long time that I felt a shred of hope that life could be different.

I was so preoccupied with my own feelings, my own messed-up life, that I scarcely thought about Elsie at all. For years, I had built up a wall around me to keep the outside world at bay, an elaborate protection system to insulate myself from the grim realities of what my life had become. So my failures as a husband were not foremost in my mind at this point. Instead, I concentrated on learning how to live my life free from alcohol. AA meetings were instrumental in restoring my self-esteem and forcing me to deal with reality. In two specific instances I credit my AA friends for helping me navigate some difficult passages.

The first instance involved finding a job. For six months, I'd been searching for a "good" job that would make me feel good about myself and make others feel proud of me. But it wasn't easy to explain my choppy employment history and my lack of employment since the suicide attempt. I failed to get a top job, and my AA friends pointed out that it was more important to work than to have an important position and big money.

Finally, I learned of a management trainee position at a bakery. The boss took one look at me, pronounced me "overqualified" and said he wouldn't hire me because I would probably not stay long. I agreed that I was overqualified, but I told him that could be a benefit to the company.

"I need this job for my own self-esteem," I told him. All the former bluff and bravado of my drinking days was absent. I mustered the courage to tell him the whole story. I summed it up by saying, "I can't promise I'll be here forever, but while I'm here, I'll be the most incredible management trainee you've ever had." He was convinced, and he assigned me to a site in Wheeling, West Virginia. I stayed there Monday through Friday and came back home on the weekends.

It felt terrific to make a fresh start. I attended AA meetings in Wheeling practically every weeknight, and that became my point of identification. My job involved learning to do all the tasks involved in bread production and then writing a paper about each position. After that I worked as a swing man, giving other people breaks. Part of the job involved what bakers call "earning your stripes." When sandwich loaves come out of the oven in their square pans, you inevitably get burn marks across your forearms when you take the lid off, even when you're wearing asbestos gloves. I wore my "stripes" proudly, because I knew I was doing the job well. I hadn't missed a day, hadn't been late and didn't need to make up excuses.

The second instance in which AA helped me indirectly occurred when the divorce became final. Even though I had not been thinking about Elsie at all, I was surprised at the depth of emotion I felt when those divorce papers were handed to me. It was on the weekend, while I was at home with Mom and Dad. Dad answered a knock on the door, and said, "Dave, it's for you."

There stood a deputy sheriff with a thick envelope in his hand. "Are you David MacKenzie?" he asked. I took the envelope from him, opened it up, and I immediately saw the line that reads "Grounds for Divorce." It stung me to read, "Divorce granted on grounds of extreme cruelty."

I looked up, and the deputy was smiling at me—leering, I thought. I didn't say a word ... just stalked upstairs. "Whatever happened to 'mutual incompatibility'?" I groused. "Why did she have to twist the knife?"

The harsh reality of Elsie's perception of what sort of husband I had been might have plunged me back into despair had it not been for the sustaining support of my AA groups and distraction of my new job. And the more I thought about it, the more I realized "extreme cruelty" was no exaggeration. As an alcoholic descends into the middle and advanced stages of the disease, nothing matters except obtaining and ingesting liquor.

Relationships—especially close family bonds—are finally painfully sacrificed. Yet all the while, the alcoholic keeps up his patter about "changing," going "on the wagon," promising "it won't happen again." Wise is the spouse who, like Elsie, calls the alcoholic's bluff and says, "I'm not going to take it any more!"

Inside the Alcoholic

In chapter two we mentioned a number of symptoms that are

indicative of alcoholism. They include an increasing tolerance for liquor, a distinct personality change on the part of the drinker and a growing preoccupation with alcohol. Alcoholics make certain liquor is readily available, no matter what they have to do to get it.

I agree with experts in the fields of medicine and addiction treatment who consider alcoholism a disease. That is a position which has stirred controversy for nearly two centuries. Yet, the evidence increasingly indicates that some people—about ten per cent of those who drink—are much more vulnerable to alcohol than others. Some scientists claim to have identified a genetic abnormality shared by many alcoholics. Others point to a cluster of physiological differences between alcoholics and nonalcoholics.

Since 1935, Alcoholics Anonymous has considered alcoholism a disease. And the American Medical Association calls alcoholism a primary, chronic, progressive and fatal disease. Simply put, alcoholism is not a symptom of a more serious condition. It will not go away on its own. Its victims keep on getting worse, and, eventually, if they are not treated, they will die.

In the early stages of the disease, alcoholics adapt to internal physical changes brought about by drinking. There is evidence that alcoholics share in common a liver enzyme malfunction that causes their bodies to process alcohol differently from others. That same liver malfunction is often present in the adult children of alcoholics—even if those children do not drink.

Another factor involves a physically based preference for alcohol. Brain chemistry, both in humans and in laboratory animals, has been shown to predict how strong a preference for alcohol a particular individual will have.

These factors help explain why some people appear to experience an instant addiction to alcohol. Even in high school, I could put away more than a dozen screwdrivers in an evening. That is an exorbitant capacity for liquor. Some alcoholics crave more alcohol to intensify and sustain their drunken "high." Right away, they have withdrawal symptoms when they stop drinking, and their tolerance level changes with the first few drinks.

Physically and psychologically for the early alcoholic, drinking is nothing but sheer pleasure. None of the bad physical effects has set in yet, and the drinker is still in control of when and how much he or she consumes.

Anyone astute enough to recognize the warning signs at this point would not likely make much progress confronting the drinker. A typical response at this stage is, "Why are you picking on me? I can drink twice as much as anyone else and still be in complete control. I don't *need* to drink, and besides, my drinking isn't causing any problems. I just like to relax once in a while with a few drinks."

With balance and harmony disrupted, a marriage relationship begins to decay, like the orbit of a satellite due to plunge back to earth. Drink becomes a comfortable haven and refuge for the alcoholic and a surefire retreat in the face of conflict or challenge. The alcoholic generally does not like to take charge, make decisions, or assume the ordinary responsibilities of being a husband or wife. So, increasingly, all the household concerns fall to the nonalcoholic spouse.

Emotional immaturity is another telltale characteristic. Instead of confronting life's difficulties and learning from them, the alcoholic slides comfortably into the warm glow of drinking and fails to master essential life skills. That was certainly true in my case. When I joined AA at age twenty-nine, they really had a big teenager on their hands. I was adept at avoiding my problems and passing them off on others—usually Elsie.

At some point, the drinker leaves the early stage of the disease and enters a middle stage, characterized by some different, and more alarming, symptoms. Gradually, the drinker shifts from enjoying liquor to craving it. Addiction sets in as the cells of his central nervous system change in such a way that they dictate a requirement for alcohol.

In this stage, according to Dr. James R. Milam and Katherine Ketcham, "the penalties of drinking begin to outweigh the benefits."[1] Actual physical withdrawal occurs if the alcoholic stops drinking, and a drinker's suffering is enormous. Milam and Ketcham conclude:

Blood vessels constrict, cutting down on the flow of blood and oxygen to the cells. The blood glucose level drops sharply and remains unstable. . . . Hormones, enzymes, and body fluid levels fluctuate erratically.

These chaotic events cause fundamental disruptions in the brain's chemical and electrical activity. . . . The brain is, in a sense, short-circuiting, and the resulting pandemonium creates numerous psychological and physiological problems for the alcoholic, including profound mental confusion, memory defects, lack of muscular coordination, convulsions, hallucinations, paranoia, violent or fearful behavior.[2]

When I stopped drinking for six months before we moved to the farmhouse in Michigan, it simply didn't work. I remained irritable, unpredictable and temperamental because my body craved alcohol. I was well into the middle stage of the disease, and I knew something was wrong. I just couldn't admit it, even to myself.

This is the stage when, for many drinkers, guilt, shame and self-hatred emerge. If they are uneducated about alcoholism, then they remain captives of society's stereotypes: they become convinced they are weak-willed, irresponsible, immoral and no longer able to take charge of their lives. They also begin experiencing a strong and terrible indicator of alcoholism: blackouts. A blackout occurs when a drinker appears to function normally, but later cannot remember anything that happened during a particular period of time.

The married alcoholic begins to hide his drinking, sneaking out to bars or literally concealing liquor, as I did, in the trunk of a car or some other obscure place. The signs of dependency are plain as day, and they trigger repeated demands from the wife that her husband "shape up." Marital problems multiply, and so do difficulties at work. Many alcoholics attempt to cope by using a "geographic cure": moving to a new town, starting a new job.

For many alcoholics their responses indicate a low tolerance for frustration. The least little annoyance drives them up a wall. And the wife, in particular, appears to the alcoholic to be utterly incompetent. The spouses begin sparring verbally, and ultimatums get tossed about.

Ironically, the more the spouse turns up the heat, the more the alcoholic turns to the bottle. Drinking is excused because of the problems drinking has caused. The alcoholic sees no contradiction in his reasoning. At the same time, though, he barricades inside himself the overwhelming guilt, self-pity and worry brought on by out-of-control drinking.

The late stages of alcoholism present a picture that is most often associated with drunkenness: the alcoholic begins drinking in the morning and continues drinking enough all day to stave off the painful symptoms of withdrawal. He sacrifices every last vestige of self-respect and marital harmony to his addiction. Physical symptoms run riot in his body, resulting in gastritis (an inflamed stomach lining), heart problems, cancer and liver failure.

The late-stage alcoholic is incapable of figuring out just how much alcohol to drink in order to keep functioning ("maintenance drinking," as it is called). Instead, he binges heavily and frequently or remains falling-down drunk most of the time. He is very unlikely to stick with his job, so he becomes financially dependent on family members or government assistance.

I do not believe that the disease of alcoholism, in my case, had run its course to this last, deteriorative stage. However, my emotional anguish was acute, and I responded in the same way many advanced alcoholics respond: with a desperate attempt to escape via suicide. A ruined marriage was not part of the picture I had envisioned as I planned my life. And the knowledge that I had driven Elsie away, little by little, day after day, for the sake of drinking hurt me as nothing had ever hurt. And so I wished desperately for a terminal illness—anything that might excuse or explain why I acted as I did. I simply had no idea, until AA got hold of me, that alcoholism was a potentially fatal disease and that it was in my power to see it arrested once and for all in my life.

Made New

There is a strong spiritual dimension to AA, and I did not

know how to assimilate that part of my recovery process into my life. I'd had no significant church experience, and here were my alcoholic friends telling me to "make a decision to turn your will and your life over to the care of God, as you understand him."

The little I knew about God told me he would not like me at all. I'd driven Elsie away, neglected my two sons and forsaken my job, all the while insisting that I was behaving rationally and normally. Trying to reconcile what I was doing with whom I thought I should be set up an unbearable internal tension that was unleashed only in the most inappropriate ways. How could I approach anything resembling God when every fiber of my being told me to run and hide from him? Besides, I told myself, I already am a Christian; it's just the same as being an American or an economist for that matter. It was a point of identification, not a relationship. Yet, just as AA lit a fire under me to get me over to Elsie's parents' home for my brief apology, AA also pointed me in the direction of a "higher power."

Obediently, I began attending the 7:45 A.M. Sunday service at St. Stephen's, mostly because it was very small, very formal and no one ever talked to me (or to anyone else, for that matter) afterward. I knew I wouldn't bump into Elsie there, either, because she always attended a later service.

I had left my job at the bakery and had begun working as a consultant for a distributor in Florida. It was about a year after Elsie had left me and I was still coping with overwhelming guilt. Based in Pittsburgh, my job required extensive travel. One evening I landed in a Sleepytime Lodge in Orlando. My career was going well, and I intended to keep it that way. After work, the others headed out for dinner or drinking, and I walked back to my hotel room.

I flipped on the television for company and to drown out the noise of trucks on the highway, and I plunged into a pile of paperwork. At 8 P.M., out of the corner of my eye, I saw Billy Graham come into view on the screen. One of his evangelistic crusades was being aired. For some reason I did not switch channels automatically as I was in the habit of doing whenever anything vaguely religious appeared on television. I paid little attention to the program for the next fifty minutes.

Then, at the very end, the crusade closed with its trademark hymn "Just As I Am." The words seared their way into my brain, and I set down my file folders. "Dave," I thought, "God wants to deal with you just the way you are. You don't have to wait until you've got everything sorted out or atoned for or whatever." I stood in the middle of my room, wearing only a pair of boxer shorts Elsie had given me one Valentine's Day long ago. They were white with big red hearts on them. And the words that have drawn so many thousands of people forward in the course of Billy Graham's remarkable ministry drew me as well. I'd heard enough from John Guest at those early Sunday services that I even had an inkling about how to pray. So I said:

Well, Lord, if you're for real, if you're really here and I'm not just talking to the walls and if you really care, then I want you to know something. I've tried to live my life and I'm terribly unhappy about how it's turned out. Even though things are going well now, I'm still empty inside. I've got to quit doing it myself. If you want my life, you can have it.

Nothing happened. I figured God would at least blow the roof off the Sleepytime Lodge or in some other way acknowledge this momentous event. Yet within several months I could look back and see some gradual changes dating from that evening. I grew more peaceful inside; at last, the person I wanted to be was going to have a chance to come to life. And at least some of the character defects so common to alcoholics no longer claimed exclusive rights to my behavior. I was less anxious about what would happen next in my life, and I began to read the Bible.

Back in Sewickley, I had been seeing Hector and Davie regularly when Elsie brought them over to my parents' home on Saturday or Sunday afternoon. We never even exchanged greetings apart from a terse confirmation of pick-up times. "Is 4:00 okay?" "Yes."

One day, there was a hint of a change. Elsie actually looked at me and paused before she hopped back into the car. "Why don't you come over to our house to play with the boys next weekend?" she asked. "It will save gas if I don't have to make a round trip each time." Not exactly a come-on, but I felt as if something had been restored. From that point on, I began going to Elsie's every Saturday at 2 P.M. to visit with my sons in their little playroom. I missed them intensely and treasured the few hours I had with them.

I don't know exactly when it first happened, but Elsie and I found ourselves sitting side by side on the sofa occasionally, watching the two preschoolers tussle over their toys. "Isn't Hector sharing a lot better than he was just a few weeks ago?" Elsie asked. "Yeah," I said, "but Davie is more assertive now too. Hector's been put in his place a few times."

There we were: divorced, and talking more like spouses

than we ever did when we were married. I had no designs on winning Elsie back. I had progressed painfully through the grief that accompanies a divorce or any other life trauma, and I had accepted the fact that the marriage was over. I had to be responsible for myself, and that was a big enough task for the moment. Second-guessing Elsie's thoughts and feelings just wasn't on my agenda.

At the same time, I was increasingly eager to talk about the Bible, and I knew Elsie had plugged into every women's group St. Stephen's had to offer. She was much further along than me in her walk with the Lord. So, after a few weeks our conversations shifted to spiritual things. I would ask questions such as, "My Bible seems to say that we should rejoice when we suffer; what does your Bible say?" I hadn't quite caught on to the fact that different translations said essentially the same thing.

Fortunately, Elsie was tolerant of my ignorance. I found myself relying on her wisdom and trusting her interpretations. That was a remarkable change from the days when I "knew it all." Our discussions about the Bible provided us with neutral, common ground on which to build communication which we never before had shared. I truly wanted to grow in my faith, and I recognized Elsie's greater knowledge.

Without intending to do so, my questions and observations were conveying respect toward her as a person. That, too, had been sorely missed in our former relationship. God had humbled me—slam-dunked me, in fact—and I was finally free to be a whole person. It was all right to be vulnerable, to ask questions and to express feelings I'd never even acknowledged before.

One Saturday afternoon, our conversation ran on toward

dinner time. "Why don't we take the boys out for something to eat?" Elsie suggested. We did, and we enjoyed ourselves. The next Saturday, Elsie lined up a babysitter, and just the two of us went out.

Our initial steps toward reconciliation took a lot of courage on Elsie's part. If ever there was a divorce in which one person wore the white hat and the other the black, ours was it. But if reconciliation is going to happen, both people have to change. Elsie had to change and so did I. She had to become a little more assertive and express her opinion. She had to learn to leave behind her codependent habits and traits. I had to change a lot and not only in terms of stopping drinking. I had to work on character defects that had built up over the past fifteen years to a debilitating point: self-centeredness, pride, ego. Only I could deal with those, but until I did a serious relationship was out of the question.

Our talks about what God was teaching us had led us to one irrefutable conclusion: both of us wanted to live lives pleasing to God. What did that mean? we wondered together. The words of 1 Corinthians 7:11 kept coming back to us and kept plaguing Elsie. Is reconciliation really possible? we began asking. Does that mean we should get remarried? We continued discussing until it reached a point where some sort of decision needed to be made. "We really need to decide," I told Elsie. "Are we going to make a go of it?"

It was a scary moment, and if it was scary for me, it must have been terrifying for Elsie. Practically everyone she knew in Sewickley would consider her a total fool for re-entering the situation she fled twelve months earlier.

Finally, John Guest got into the act. "Don't do this yourselves," he counseled. "Let God be at work in your relationship." And he had some practical advice as well. "Get some good, Christian marriage counseling now," he said. "Keep your hands off each other, court one another and do it right this time."

The American secular dating system that we had followed in our first courtship is fundamentally opposed to Christian dating. In the secular system, the goal is to present a picture of yourself that will impress and please the other person. You try to win the object of your affection, emphasizing your good points and hiding your weak points. So you dress up, mind your manners and take your date to things that you know she likes.

The goal of Christian dating is to discover if this is the person that God wants you to marry. Therefore, you try to get to know everything about her that you can and let her know everything about you ... weaknesses included. You try to become transparent to each other.

So in our second courtship I took Elsie to places that she had never been before, where she was not comfortable, so I could learn how she reacted to unusual situations. One evening I took her to see professional wrestling at the Civic Arena in Pittsburgh.

As the controlled psychology of the evening unfolded, a lady sitting behind us told Bruno Sammartino loudly and graphically what she thought he should do to his opponent (in four-letter language that I hadn't heard since boot camp in the Marine Corps). Elsie did not get ruffled; I saw a new tenacity in her and my respect for her increased. At the same time, I had to admit to her that I felt uncomfortable, that I was offended by the lady's language.

Being transparent to each other felt good, but—again—it

was *very* scary. It meant taking risks and risking rejection, but I had to do it. I had pledged myself to seek God's will for my life, not my own, so "winning" Elsie back through the usual mechanics of dating would have been a failure. We were seeking, instead, a confirmation of God's choice for our lives.

Three months after we began dating seriously, we got engaged. John had just become rector of St. Stephen's, and we made an appointment with him to discuss our wedding plans. "I have a wonderful idea," he told us. "The two of you could get remarried during a Sunday morning worship service, and the other couples there could renew their vows." We were open to that. If God could use us to strengthen somebody else, that would be terrific.

Changes in my life were occurring swiftly like time-lapse photography of a wound healing. It would be easy to say that God wrought a miracle in me overnight—easy, but wrong. Certainly, God was active in my life. And clearly, he is the one who engineered my reconciliation with Elsie. But the hard work of recovery was my task. Even the most apparently hopeless victim of alcoholism can change, even in the latest stages of the disease. The stakes are very high ... nothing less than life and death. And the requirements of a successful journey toward recovery are exceedingly demanding. Understanding what goes into treatment and recovery is the focus of the next chapter.

CHAPTER 5

Finding Help

*W*hen I was eleven years old, my grandfather MacKenzie gave me an old, abandoned 1927 Chevy flatbed truck. It stayed on his eighty-acre orange grove ranch in California, and every summer I spent hours tinkering with it while I visited my grandparents. That old truck was a beauty (in my eyes, at least), but getting it to run took some serious intervention.

First, I had to hook it up to a tractor and tow it awhile to get it started. That procedure usually worked, but my crude towing procedure bent the front bumper out of line so far that it blocked the wheels from turning. After the engine settled into a relatively reliable purr, I had to unhitch the truck from the tractor and take a sledgehammer to the front bumper, forcing it back into shape.

All that aggravation didn't matter to me, though, because I loved my truck. Any amount of effort was worth it to me to finally sit behind the wheel and have that truck respond as I drove it. As I think about alcoholism treatment and recovery, I'm often reminded of that truck.

An alcoholic can be every bit as recalcitrant about entering treatment as that old truck was about starting its engine. The bottom line is this: left to their own devices, neither that flatbed Chevy nor an alcoholic can get going. In virtually every case of successful alcoholism recovery, the process is jump-started from the outside. This step comes before an alcoholic joins AA. I do not usually recommend starting the recovery process in AA, although I did it that way. The focus of AA is on maintaining long-term sobriety and working on negative character traits that have grown to exaggerated proportions because of problem drinking.

There is a process known as "intervention." It is the tractor that tows the addict into treatment. AA is the driving instructor that helps keep the old truck running smoothly and on the right side of the road.

Intervention is an event planned by a treatment professional in consultation with a spouse (or other family member) who wants to seek lasting help for the alcoholic. It consists of a meeting between the alcoholic, the treatment professional, and any relatives or friends selected to participate. In a loving but firm manner, they confront the alcoholic with specific evidence of the disease and urge a decision to enter treatment. Sadly, this sort of clinical intervention is often a long time in coming. Confrontation is painful, and confronting the alcoholic, along with the others outside the family, means breaking the silence, shattering the façade of normalcy and admitting a very big problem. As we have mentioned throughout this book, the alcoholic's denial of having a problem is often aided and abetted by the spouse.

Before any sort of planned intervention is contemplated, the spouse may vacillate between feeling sorry for (and protective of) the alcoholic and wanting desperately to change things. Frequently, the result is a "crisis intervention." It is very different from the clinical intervention described above. Here I'll tell what happens when a spouse opts for crisis intervention.

When Elsie believed I was serious about suicide one time, she called the police. At another point, when I failed to come home and Elsie was frantic, she telephoned her dad. Both of these examples of crisis intervention are aimed at solving an immediate problem caused by alcoholism: in the first case, keeping me from shooting myself and, in the second, seeking consolation in the face of terrifying uncertainty.

Crisis intervention does not have any goal apart from easing the immediate pain brought on by the consequences of problem drinking. It's a natural and very understandable outburst on the part of a spouse filled with frustration and anger. It frequently crops up in the midst of other doomed attempts to deal with alcoholism, such as the "geographic cure" of starting over by changing jobs or neighborhoods.

As the disease of alcoholism progresses, the spouse faces two choices: either maintain the family secret at all costs until the alcoholic hits bottom or seek outside professional help. Fortunately, help is more readily available today than it ever has been, thanks to people such as Betty Ford. By speaking and writing about her own battle with chemical dependency, and by founding one of the nation's most well-respected treatment centers, Mrs. Ford has shed new light on the realities of addiction and recovery.

The spouse who chooses clinical intervention by seeking outside help may experience some powerful and scary feelings at first. Isn't she being disloyal—even sneaky—to go behind her husband's back like this? How can she come to terms with her own participation in the alcoholic's disease? Can she gain enough emotional distance from him to tell him the truth, objectively and without judging?

I've often wondered how I would have responded to a formal intervention if Elsie had planned one. By the time I left the farm to take my "road trip" to D.C., I was so desperate that I believe I would have been willing to try anything. I would have been angry and would have balked at everything that was said, but I think I would have been persuaded to enter treatment. I knew something was terribly wrong.

As it happened, there was no intervention before I hit bottom. Only because of that neighbor boy, a competent medical detoxification program and my ready acceptance of AA was the cycle of addiction broken for me. It is crucial to understand this: a planned intervention in the life of an alcoholic before he hits bottom is vastly better than what I went through.

Intervention could save years of grief, keep a marriage intact and, literally, save a life. Many alcoholics do reach a point where suicide appears to be the only way out. Intervention does not work 100 per cent of the time, but it is the best method yet developed for beginning the recovery process. Even if it does not work, the time and effort put into it are far from wasted.

With intervention, family members who participate are changed forever, because they have faced up to the problem and have decided to do something about it. They know they are not alone. Friends and relatives know what they're going through and want to help. And according to experts in the field, a second or third try at intervention will frequently succeed as the alcoholic's defenses gradually wear down. One thing is certain: it works best when the alcoholic's support system—his marriage, his job, his friends—is still there for him.

Don't Go It Alone

What happens if that support network is not firmly in place or if you decide to attempt an intervention without careful planning and assistance from a professional? I learned the hard way that this sort of "informal" intervention is less likely to succeed.

On two occasions I attempted an intervention with my alcoholic mother. The first attempt came when I was visiting her alone one time, several years after I remarried Elsie. As always, Mom carried with her an eight-ounce glass filled with clear liquid and an ice cube. It was vodka with a drop of water in it. She would frequently attempt to hide it when other people were around. Mom was a "maintenance drinker," meaning she sipped alcohol all day long and remained fairly alert and functional. She was not a binge drinker, as I was.

I had planned to confront her, and seeing her alcoholic behavior play out over the course of one morning strengthened my resolve. I had invited my father to be present as well, but he refused. He said, "I'll support you, but I can't be there." So I was on my own. I opened with a nonthreatening line: "Why don't you sit down, Mom, you are getting a little shaky. Maybe you should take a nap."

Her feathers began ruffling instantly. "What do you mean?" she asked.

"Mom, you have been drinking and you are not sober right now." At that, she went into high dudgeon.

"I have not been drinking!" she said, emphasizing every word as she steadied herself against a sofa. "I haven't had a drink for a long time."

I tried to keep a steady, nonjudgmental tone in my voice. "Mom, you carry it around with you all the time. You were drinking not more than fifteen minutes ago."

"I haven't had a drink all day," she said vehemently. So I asked, "Would you believe me if I put your drink in your hand?" I led her into the kitchen, reached into the cupboard, pulled out her "water" glass, and placed it in her hand. The ice in it had not even melted.

"Gosh, that must have been in there a long time," she said. Her ability to persistently deny what she was doing even while holding the glass in her hand was remarkable, but not all that unusual. We stayed in that kitchen for no less than four hours, sparring over every detail of what alcoholism and chemical dependency were doing to her. I was terrified, yet I kept hammering away, forcing her to face the evidence. In the end she was sobbing; we were both sitting on the kitchen floor, and I was holding her.

"I do have a problem," she said. "I'll go someplace as long as it's away from here." I got on the phone to John L. immediately, and he recommended a twenty-eight-day program in Reading, Pennsylvania. She dutifully went to the program, and stuck with it until the end. Dad was very supportive, visiting her on the weekends. When she returned home, I arranged for some ladies from AA to visit her, and they faithfully paid calls and got to know her.

For three months she was in great shape. It was a pleasure to see her, and we could drop in anytime, laugh and tell jokes and not worry about whether she was about to blow up. Then, because she thought her counselor had insulted or slighted her, she began drinking again. She convinced herself that she did not have a problem with alcoholism. "I just went overboard a little," she said. In no time, she was right back into it, gripping her vodka glass firmly in hand, telling herself that the problem was minor and that she could control it.

Just two years before she died, my brother Alan and I tried again to get her into treatment. She agreed to check into a hospital in Pittsburgh, but she checked herself out after three days. In October 1988, she died of internal organ failure brought on by alcoholism.

When Intervention Works

Vernon E. Johnson, founder of the Johnson Institute in Minneapolis, is widely recognized as an authority on the treatment of chemical dependency, beginning with planned intervention. I am indebted to his book, *Intervention*, for explaining how the intervention process works.

It begins with a decision, usually on the part of a spouse (but sometimes a son, daughter or employer), to confront the alcoholic with irrefutable evidence of his or her addiction. The confrontation is done, not in anger, but out of love. It is intended to break down the alcoholic's solid wall of denial, present him with the reality of how drinking is wrecking his life and offer him a chance to enter a specific treatment program as soon as the intervention ends.

I have been involved in several interventions, but I am no expert at planning and arranging them. If a counselee, such as Christine from chapter one, made the decision to intervene in her husband's alcoholism, I would refer her to a trained professional at a treatment center. Often, these are affiliated with hospitals. Let's take a look at how Christine's first visit might proceed, with an intervention specialist named Mr. Pearson. Christine explains why she made an appointment:

> I'm feeling really desperate about my husband, Bill. He can't seem to stop drinking no matter where he is or what he's doing, and he always ends up drunk. I've been reading about alcoholism, and I believe Bill fits all the symptoms . . . too perfectly. What can I do to help him?

Mr. Pearson:

> If you are willing to plan an intervention, that is the best way to get Bill into treatment now, before he deteriorates any further. Let me explain what happens in an intervention. First, could you make a list of the people Bill knows well and trusts?

Christine:

> Well, there's his boss, Mr. Atkins; and his sister Louisa lives here in town. His parents are out in California, and we don't see them very often.

Mr. Pearson:

> Do you think Mr. Atkins and Louisa know Bill has a drinking problem? Have you discussed it with them?

Christine:

> Oh, yes. Louisa needles him about it every chance she gets. And I've talked with Mr. Atkins more times than I can

count, calling in sick for Bill. I can tell Mr. Atkins doesn't believe me anymore. And last week, when I phoned in for Bill, Mr. Atkins told me Bill was overdrawn on sick days by a long shot. He said Bill ought to get some professional help. That's one of the reasons I believe we need to do an intervention.

Mr. Pearson:

Okay. Let me explain what we will do next. It's very important that these plans be kept secret from Bill. He must not know about the intervention ahead of time. We'll schedule a meeting with Louisa and Mr. Atkins, and ask them to write down specific instances when they have observed Bill's drinking affecting his ability to function.

Meanwhile, tell Louisa not to "needle" him anymore. That just makes him more defensive and more resistant to the reality he needs to acknowledge. And don't try to interfere with his drinking; don't pour any liquor down the drain or badger him about late nights. By the way, do you have a camcorder?

Christine:

"No, but Louisa does. Why?"

Mr. Pearson:

The point of the intervention is to present the facts in such a way that Bill can no longer deny what alcohol is doing to him. One of the most effective ways to do that is to shoot some videotape of him when he's at his worst, perhaps at a party or a business function after he's overdone it at the bar. See if you can borrow the camera and capture him live and in color.

At the next meeting, Mr. Pearson reviews the goals of the intervention and asks each participant to read some of the remembered incidents about Bill. Mr. Pearson tells Christine, Louisa and Mr. Atkins that he will be running the intervention; he will come with them and direct each one to speak in turn, probably beginning with Christine.

Mr. Pearson also raises a disheartening "what-if." If Bill will not enter treatment after the intervention, Mr. Pearson says, then Christine and Mr. Atkins ought to be prepared to carry out additional actions to force Bill to confront his disease. This may mean going through with a trial separation and lining up a place for Christine to stay; or it might mean a valid threat by Mr. Atkins to fire Bill from his job. The group schedules one more meeting to rehearse what will be said and how. Mr. Pearson emphasizes the need to affirm Bill throughout the intervention and not attack him. Christine gathers information about three treatment programs recommended by Mr. Pearson and selects one at a nearby hospital. She makes a reservation for Bill to enter a twenty-eight-day course of treatment, beginning the afternoon of the intervention.

Finally, the day arrives. Louisa has invited Bill and Christine to her home, ostensibly for dinner. When they get there, Bill is shocked to see Mr. Atkins in the living room, sitting next to a stranger in a gray suit.

"Bill, I'd like you to meet Mr. Pearson," says Christine. "We're going to have dinner a little later, but for now we need to talk with you. Mr. Pearson will explain."

Bill is visibly shaken and begins to protest. "What is this, a surprise party? Are you trying to trick me into something?" Mr. Pearson steps in and asks Bill to take a seat. He says, "Bill, your sister, your boss and your wife all care about you very deeply. All we ask is that you listen for a few minutes.

Christine will begin."

Before Christine can say a word from her prepared introduction, Bill has caught on. "It's my drinking, isn't it? You all think I have a problem. Well, why don't you go pick on someone who *really* abuses alcohol? I mean the guys who are out weaving all over the road at night; the ones who can't even hold down a job." Christine skips her introduction and moves right into the specific instances she has written down.

"Bill, last Friday night you *were* weaving all over the road. You drank more than half-a-dozen martinis at Sam's retirement party, and I finally drove home after you ran the car up on the curb.

"And, Bill, I'm not saying these things to be cruel. I want you to get better. You have a disease, and it's nothing to be ashamed of. I've been doing a lot of reading about alcoholism, and with treatment, you can be just fine again."

Christine draws a deep breath, and Bill remains silent. So Christine carries on with incident after incident: empty bottles in the trash, Bill's inability to keep up with simple chores like lawn mowing and car washing. She hands him a stack of canceled checks which show how much Bill is spending on liquor.

Bill fidgets in his chair; he turns to Mr. Atkins and says:
Do you buy into this too? Isn't Christine overreacting just a bit here? I do my job just fine; in fact, you guys couldn't get along without me.

Mr. Atkins rubs his forehead, clears his throat and says:
Bill, my records show you've called in sick eight times this month. Every month it gets worse. And your lunchtime drinking is legendary. When we took that new client out last Wednesday, you were on your third glass of wine

before our entrees were served. The rest of the day, you just couldn't function. In fact, you fell asleep at your desk for about forty minutes.

When Louisa's turn comes, she dims the lights and flicks on the television. "Now what?" says Bill. "Did you rent some goody-two-shoes documentary about not drinking?" Bill stops talking abruptly as he sees himself appear on the screen, attending a block party in Louisa's neighborhood the week before last.

There he is with a can of beer in one hand, talking too loudly to a group of guys. One by one, as the camera rolls, the men wander away from the group. Then Bill starts talking right into the camera. His voice is slurred, and the story he is telling rambles on nonsensically. When Louisa turns up the lights, Bill is staring grimly at the floor.

Christine breaks the silence.

Bill, you've got to get help. I've made a reservation for you at Baptist Hospital's treatment program. Your suitcase is all packed and in the car. We can go there right after dinner.

Bill is shocked.

I don't need to go to a hospital. I can quit drinking anytime I want to! I'll quit right now. You've shown me my problem; now I'll take care of it.

Mr. Pearson gently breaks in.

Bill, you need to understand that dependency on alcohol is a chronic disease like diabetes. The recovery process is not easy and it takes time. The best way to begin is with a medical program.

Bill protests again, saying he can't miss work. "Mr. Atkins just told me I've been absent too much!"

Mr. Atkins has a ready reply.

I've arranged to split your work between Chuck and Linda for the next month. If you go into treatment today, your job will be waiting for you when you come out.

Finally, Bill has no more excuses to offer. And no one has said anything to plunge him into rage or self-pity. Even Louisa is talking to him in a way that doesn't infuriate him. Mr. Pearson and Mr. Atkins leave the house, and Bill eats in silence with Christine and Louisa. Afterwards, he and Christine get in the car and drive to the hospital. Christine tells him:

Our marriage is too precious to waste. I want you to be the husband and father you used to be, before alcohol got hold of you. I'll come and visit as often as I can. Things are going to be so much better. You'll see.

What's Next?

At a hospital or an in-patient treatment center, the alcoholic begins by undergoing detoxification. After a thorough examination, the patient begins a slow and often painful withdrawal from alcohol addiction. This can be eased by medication and controlled nutrition.

Withdrawal generally takes three or four days, and there are some treatment centers that will release a patient at that point, when he or she is said to have "dried out." In the vast majority of these cases the drinker gets drunk again . . . and soon. Surviving withdrawal is not enough. Arresting the physiological effects of the disease does not produce sobriety. More is required. In an effective treatment program, medical attention is followed up with education, group therapy and participation in Alcoholics Anonymous. All these aspects of treatment and recovery have a single goal: equipping the alcoholic to manage the disease by never drinking again.

Education is crucial because alcoholics fall prey to societal myths about the disease. More than likely they have come to believe they are worthless, abnormal, immoral and unsalvageable. Group sessions work wonders. They introduce alcoholics to people from all walks of life who suffer just as they do. According to Vernon Johnson:

These are no-nonsense, confrontive, and sometimes painful times. The wall of defenses doesn't just crack; it breaks down and stays down as a result of the caring interaction of fellow patients and staff.[1]

While the walls of defense and denial are tumbling, a new foundation is carefully put in place. Alcoholics are encouraged and praised, and they come to recognize positive traits about themselves. The normal course of growth and maturity, arrested by alcohol, is set in motion again. Discovering good things about themselves permits alcoholics to plan and dream about the future. A strong sense of self-worth affords powerful incentive to stay sober.

Individual growth and stability are crucial, but they are not enough. Once the alcoholic emerges from treatment, clear-eyed, cleaned up and free of the toxic physical effects of alcohol, he or she has a moral obligation to avoid alcohol completely. Drinking "moderately" or "socially" remains every bit as impossible for the alcoholic now as it was when he was in the death-grip of alcohol addiction.

Staying sober long-term takes effort and ongoing support. That is the business of Alcoholics Anonymous. Virtually every alcoholism treatment specialist, counselor, doctor and a vast majority of recovering alcoholics credit AA with keeping more than a million alcoholics off the bottle. The organization is unparalleled in its commitment to alcoholism recovery and its effectiveness in keeping people sober.

Alcoholics Anonymous

In 1935, a former New York stockbroker and a surgeon from Akron, Ohio, found they had something in common: they were both considered "hopeless" alcoholics. Together, they discovered they could help one another stay sober. With the help of an Episcopal priest named Samuel Shoemaker, they developed a set of spiritual principles to follow. These principles, known as the "Twelve Steps," proved helpful to other alcoholics as well. The Twelve Steps are biblically based, yet they are applicable to people of any religion (or none) as long as they want to stop drinking. The steps are:

1. We admitted we were powerless over alcohol—that our lives had become unmanageable.

2. Came to believe that a Power greater than ourselves could restore us to sanity.

3. Made a decision to turn our will and our lives over to the care of God, as we understood Him.

4. Made a searching and fearless moral inventory of ourselves.

5. Admitted to God, to ourselves, and to another human being the exact nature of our wrongs.

6. Were entirely ready to have God remove all these defects of character.

7. Humbly asked Him to remove our shortcomings.

8. Made a list of all persons we had harmed, and became willing to make amends to them all.

9. Made direct amends to such people wherever possible,

except when to do so would injure them or others.

10. Continued to take personal inventory and when we were wrong promptly admitted it.

11. Sought through prayer and meditation to improve our conscious contact with God as we understood Him, praying only for knowledge of His will for us and the power to carry that out.

12. Having had a spiritual awakening as the result of these steps, we tried to carry this message to alcoholics and to practice these principles in all our affairs.

Today, AA is a self-supporting affiliation of groups and chapters throughout the world. It is headquartered in New York, and it remains unaligned with any church, ideology or political position. The only requirements for membership are these: you must be an alcoholic, and you must want to stop drinking.

In a few instances alcoholics have begun their process of treatment and recovery in AA. This is very risky, however, because without medical attention and detoxification, the alcoholic is likely to experience great suffering and find himself more vulnerable to a relapse. Most often, AA participation begins while an alcoholic is still undergoing a twenty-eight-day course of treatment. AA groups frequently meet at treatment centers. This helps newly sober members feel a sense of belonging and acceptance before they return home.

The AA philosophy encourages alcoholics to live life "one day at a time." The commitment never to drink requires day-to-day renewal as well. A participant in AA would never say, "I am not going to drink for the rest of my life." They would be encouraged to say, "I'm not going to drink today." And if a day is too long, then the alcoholic vows to stop drinking for one hour, or for ten minutes.

The lure of drinking remains, because all the old cues are still in place when the alcoholic goes home. "Here comes trouble, where's the bottle?" is practically a reflexive response, even after treatment. And doctors have found it takes two years before the full physical effects of alcohol disappear from the body.

When an alcoholic begins to participate in AA, he is usually encouraged to attend ninety meetings in ninety days. Thereafter, attending meetings once or twice a week is considered sufficient. Clearly, being active in AA draws the alcoholic away from home a lot, and that might not be too popular with a spouse who does not understand the goals and purpose of the group. Spouses may attend AA's open meetings where alcoholics speak about their experiences. They also should link up with Al-Anon, as described in chapter three. That way, they have a place to find support as well. Also, their understanding of what the alcoholic and his family goes through is deepened.

Along with open meetings, AA offers "closed" meetings as well. In some of these sessions the twelve steps of recovery are reviewed one at a time, and participants discuss their progress—or lack of it—in carrying out the steps. Only alcoholics are permitted at these small meetings.

How AA Helps Change Lives

Often, people who are unfamiliar with the organization attach a stereotypical stigma to AA. They tend to believe it is a gathering place for wild-eyed degenerates with no place better to go. I certainly didn't relish the idea of showing up at an open meeting—one that is held in a public place and not restricted.

Yet I knew I had to go. The next open meeting was scheduled for a Monday evening at St. Stephen's. Monday was a warm, sunny day, yet I bundled up in a raincoat and hat before I left for the church. I parked in an obscure spot a couple blocks away and did my best to sneak into the meeting. I didn't want anyone to see me going into *that* room with *those* people!

At that meeting, newcomers were asked to stand and introduce themselves. I wasn't ready to do so, and I believed it violated AA's fundamental principle of anonymity. I did not return to an open meeting for a while, but I continued meeting with the group that had gathered at John's house.

It was in the setting of a closed meeting at my friend John L.'s home that I made the commitment to "make amends" to Elsie's parents, out of obedience to Steps 8 and 9. Knowing that my AA friends stood behind me—and would ask me how it went—motivated me to do something I would never have done on my own.

Similarly, AA was instrumental in planting the seed of personal faith in my life. My commitment to Jesus Christ came after I had been participating regularly in AA for nearly one year. I recognized AA's "Higher Power" as Jesus Christ, thanks in large part to John Guest's preaching and that televised altar call by Billy Graham.

There are two opposite and (I believe) equally untrue criticisms directed toward the spiritual aspects of alcoholism recovery. On the one hand, some treatment experts and some in AA itself are beginning to de-emphasize the value of spiritual renewal. They see it as an archaic throwback to

AA's early post-Prohibition days.

I believe that the truth of God's Word and God's plan for human redemption should not be amended in the name of any other "good," including alcoholism recovery. That's not the way Sam Shoemaker would have wanted it. It has been my experience that the vast majority of alcoholics who have been helped by AA recognize the centrality of spiritual renewal and growth.

At the same time, Christians who reject the disease model of alcoholism tend to assert that the alcoholic needs to repent, receive forgiveness and "sin no more." Each of these elements is crucial, and they are clearly reflected in the Twelve Steps. Yet, by themselves, they are not enough.

It is not a person's character defects or sin nature that causes him to drink abnormally; instead, the person's physical vulnerability to alcohol unleashes the worst in him. Maturity is arrested, built-in inhibitions crumble and negative character traits are magnified. Nowhere do these results of alcoholism hit harder than in the marriage. As the alcoholic sees the relationship closest to him wither and die, his resulting sense of grief and shame and worthlessness leave him distant from God, if he ever thought about God to begin with.

This is the point at which the church, in cooperation with a caring spouse and an AA program, can make a significant difference. It is no secret that the church can help marriages flourish. One of the most important contributions the church makes is to combat a sense of isolation, that numbing, frightening sensation that no one else understands what a couple is going through.

Particularly when alcoholism is involved, keeping isolation

at bay is crucial. The way in which one church did it right is detailed by Dr. Anderson Spickard, Jr., an alcoholism expert at Vanderbilt University Medical Center:

> The wife of a member came to the church asking for help because her husband was an alcoholic. The church investigated his problem, collected money to send him for treatment, mailed him get-well cards, prayed for him every day, and finally welcomed him home with a tremendous celebration. The recovering alcoholic was greeted as a prodigal son, as a man who was once blind and now could see.
>
> Because this man was fortunate enough to have a loving, caring wife and congregation helping him on the road to recovery, today he is one of the most enthusiastic and productive servants of Jesus I have ever met.[2]

I am convinced that the Holy Spirit is at work today in AA, and in even the most secularized alcoholism treatment programs. Christians who allow their preconceived notions about alcoholics to thwart the progress of treatment or the Twelve-Step program might get in the way of what God is trying to do in the life of the alcoholic.

The success rate of intervention, treatment and long-term follow-up care in the form of AA participation speaks for itself. Vernon E. Johnson, the pioneer of the intervention process, says the rate of success ranges from fifty to eighty per cent, depending on how thoroughly motivated the alcoholic and his family are and what sort of treatment program they use.[3]

A Restored Relationship
After I became a Christian, my need to stay active in AA did

not diminish. AA was my lifeline throughout the weekdays I spent in Wheeling working for the bakery. There, I attended meetings practically every evening. I chose a "buddy," a man whose recovery from alcoholism had begun about the same time mine had. The AA meetings provided a strong, responsive network of support and accountability. By spending time with a sponsor (John L., in my case), my buddy and alcoholics who telephoned for help out of sheer desperation, I learned many lessons about alcoholism and about myself.

One of the most disturbing and life-changing AA experiences I had in Wheeling involved what are known as "Twelve-Step Calls." Local volunteers from AA would take turns answering a "Hotline" telephone. Whenever an alcoholic would call in desperate for help, two or three volunteers (like me) would go out to his or her house and talk about how AA could help.

The first two times I went out to visit alcoholics who had called for help, I was astounded to see events unfold as they did. I stood outside the door, knocked a couple times, then talked quietly with the person who accompanied me on the visit. Before anyone answered the door, a single gunshot sounded from inside. Both times, the alcoholic killed himself before we could even get inside to talk.

Jarred by the sounds and sights of suicide, the memory of swallowing all those pills back at the Michigan farmhouse flooded me with painful, half-forgotten images. In the whirl of confusion emanating from rescue squad efforts, police sirens, curious neighbors gathering, I felt a sense of unreality and profound gratitude. That wasn't me being lifted on the stretcher and carried away; but only six months before, it might have been.

My life was spared, and AA entered the picture even before I'd had the brains or the courage to call them. It's important to emphasize that AA, to me and to most other recovering alcoholics, is not just an organization. It's a particular individual or two who firmly and patiently walk with the alcoholic through the steps of recovery. To me, nobody personifies the spirit of AA better than my sponsor, John L.

He probably had no interest whatsoever in attending that cocktail party in Sewickley—the one my parents dragged me to after my failed suicide attempt. As it happens, John is an old friend of Elsie's parents. They had urged him to go to the party, find me, and help me if he could.

John lost no time in telling me he was an alcoholic, and at the first hint of my willingness to keep listening, he urged me to come to that closed meeting at his home. From that time on, he continued to check on me, seek me out and schedule time to spend with me as I figured out what it meant to walk through AA's Twelve Steps. He also played a crucial role in restoring my relationship with Elsie.

One day shortly after I had apologized to Elsie's parents, John gave Elsie a call. He wanted to stop by and see her and explain what alcoholism had done to her husband. Elsie agreed to see him, even though by that time she wanted me completely erased from her life and memory. John brought along some AA and Al-Anon literature for her and talked about my progress in AA. Elsie was polite and cool toward him, she remembers. She was glad to have some additional information about the condition, she told John, and if Dave was doing well, that was fine with her.

I believe Elsie's perspective was altered, ever so slightly, by John's visit and her willingness to read up on the disease. By learning about alcoholism, and by separating herself from a disastrous marriage, Elsie gained objectivity and perspective. From the earliest days of our separation, I believe God placed in her path a whole series of steppingstones leading right back into a marriage she had forsaken forever.

This didn't happen because we are "special" or particularly gifted. On the contrary, I cannot imagine any relationship being severed with such finality. As I counsel spouses like Christine, I tell them to remain open-minded to the ways in which God may want to work in their lives. There is no telling how or when a relationship may be restored, whether or not it has succumbed to divorce. If a spouse detects any hint of a possibility of reconciliation within marriage or after marriage, then that option deserves serious consideration. As Elsie and I have been discovering, the rewards are tremendous and exciting, even though the challenges are formidable.

CHAPTER 6

Rebuilding a Marriage Relationship

Dave and Elsie became reacquainted gradually, while they *watched their two boys play together during Dave's weekend visits. The changes in Dave were so striking that Elsie had to convince herself, over and over, that he wasn't simply putting on a very good act to win her back and then let himself slip back into his old drinking habits.*

Learning to trust again didn't come easily. Every so often, Elsie would test Dave, just to see if he had really let go of their past relationship. On one particularly snowy Saturday, while he visited with the boys, Elsie bustled around the house getting ready to run an errand. "I need to pick up a dress at the cleaners," she told Dave. "I need it for a party I'm going to tonight."

Did he catch that last part? Elsie thought to herself, "Yes, former husband, I do have a social life!" *She watched him out of the corner of her eye, and was relieved to see no inkling of jealousy, disapproval or even disappointment.*

Dave hopped up from the sofa and grabbed his coat. "The weather's so lousy," he said. "Why don't you let me go pick up your dress while you stay with the boys?" That certainly was not the old Davé speaking, Elsie thought. Something was radically different.

Elsie was amazed to find herself feeling a whole lot less detached from Dave than she had been only months earlier. She picks up the story here with a give-and-take that surprised them both.

Dave had found a new job, similar to his other management positions. It would keep him on the road all week and home for the weekends. He asked whether that would be all right with me. My initial thought was, "Why should I care where you work or when you work?" Yet I found I did care. I preferred to have him in town so we could see each other, and I told him. In truth, I had been enjoying his company more than I'd let on.

And, as I have already mentioned, I kept encountering scriptural views of marriage and divorce through Bible studies and women's groups at church. A strong biblical preference for reconciliation seemed plain as day, yet I had such a difficult time accepting it and applying it to my life.

I'd been taking notes throughout the Bible studies and various women's retreats I attended. I pored over them as I read my Bible at night, wondering what the Lord had to say to a divorced Christian woman. "God wants your marriage to work," I had written. Following that was a series of steps that helped turn my mind toward positive thoughts about reconciling with Dave. They may be useful to you as well, especially if you have stayed together through the trial of alcoholism.

1. Set realistic, not idealistic, goals for your relationship. Two different people are meant to be different.

2. Take time alone together on a regular basis.

3. Talk to each other about your relationship, not to other people.

4. Look to the husband as the spiritual leader of the home.

5. Learn to accept your husband as he is, faults and all.

6. Begin to encourage him.

7. When there are problems, get counseling together.

8. Deal with sources of conflict or resentment as they arise. Don't let them stew.

What I was learning, and only gradually came to accept, was this: God doesn't reward us with a perfect husband because we're doing everything right. Instead, as we learn how to deal with a difficult, angry man, God will mold us to the image of Christ. And he will use our testimony to help others.

Throughout this entire period of preparation, Dave never pushed or pressured me to get back together. That, to me, was proof that he was attending AA for his own sake. He was not out to impress anyone. He just wanted to stick with his commitment to abstain from alcohol.

Looking back, it is easy to see how God protected us from other relationships and kept us free for one another, even when we were inclined to date around. I'll never forget a Bible study meeting in my home with John and Kathie

Guest. As the meeting ended, a single guy from my neighborhood showed up at the door, ready to pick me up for a date. Just as he came in the door, the telephone rang. John Guest answered it and beckoned me to the phone with a booming voice. "Elsie, guess who's on the phone? *Dave.*" I sighed and took the call; meanwhile, the Guests shooed my date out the door. He left and never called back.

Gradually, as Dave and I became reacquainted, we discovered a new basis for our relationship. I began telling him about my activities at St. Stephen's and about my faith. He began telling me about AA meetings and the Twelve Steps. He actually listened to me and he truly cared about the boys. I finally had to admit to myself that I was sorry to see him go each week. That was a scary feeling, because our marriage had been so horrible.

Finally, we sat next to one another on my sofa one evening. The boys were asleep, and the house was perfectly quiet. Dave broke the silence with a question that put him at real risk of rejection: "Do you think you still love me?"

I responded carefully, not wanting to sound overly eager. In truth I had never been able to put Dave out of my mind. The spark of love that was lit on a long-ago Fourth of July still burned, even though it had been virtually smothered beneath the debris of alcoholism. And my conversion to Christ strengthened and confirmed my feelings. God, I had learned, is in the business of restoring fallen human beings to himself and restoring relationships between people as well.

That was the first time we seriously discussed the possibility of remarrying. He was more interested in it than I was, but we both had a growing sense that God wanted us to get back together.

We both wondered, "What if?" What if Dave starts drinking again? What if I leave him again? Our circumstances were unique, because we had ended our marriage and then put the pieces back together. Yet the questions we faced before we remarried, and the challenges we still face to rebuild our relationship, are common to any marriage struggling with one spouse's alcoholism.

Even when divorce does not occur—and it is often avoided when the spouse married to an alcoholic seeks help early on—the marriage still needs rebuilding. Both marriage partners need to come to grips with completely altered lifestyles and ways of relating to one another. Like so many wives of alcoholic husbands, I had to break free from my pride and justifiable doubts and fears. In my mind I was cast as the heroine of the whole affair, and Dave was the bad guy. Forgiveness was not instantaneous, nor was it easy. And Dave had to continue coping with feelings of low self-esteem and worthlessness. Every so often as we courted one another again, he would sheepishly ask, "You still love me, don't you?"

Dave's answer to the question that weighed so heavily on me and on my parents ("What if he drinks again?") reflected AA's philosophy of taking alcoholism recovery one day at a time. "I can't promise that I will never drink again," he told me, "but I can promise that I will not drink today." That may sound less than completely reassuring, but it is a realistic expression of the attitude recovering alcoholics are urged to cultivate. And my parents and I had been talking regularly to John L., who told us he believed Dave's commitment to sobriety was genuine.

Dave worried that I might leave him again—whether or not he returned to drinking. But both of us drew strength from sound teaching at church and the support of Christian friends. We felt confident that if God wanted us remarried, then somehow we had to trust him through it.

Our second wedding took place April 16, 1972, in St. Stephen's huge contemporary sanctuary. There were celebration candles on the altar, but apart from those there were no special decorations. My dress was fringed at the hemline, so Dave—eager to break the tension—called me his "frayed bride." We processed down the aisle together and exchanged new vows.

After that, all the husbands and wives present in the congregation stood and faced one another. They repeated their vows in turn, following John Guest's lead. As we recessed out of the church with John, the congregation sang "Love Divine, All Loves Excelling." I cannot think of a more appropriate hymn for the occasion. The love God had shown us, even before we knew him or cared about him, was overwhelming. It is in the context of God's enormous love for us that human love flourishes and lasts.

We flew to Miami that night en route to a five-day honeymoon in Jamaica. I truly felt like a bride, far more so than I had in 1966. Before our first wedding, sex had become a stale routine; now, after two years apart and a three-month courtship without sex, making love was a new adventure and a sacred time of togetherness. I believe God blessed our physical relationship the second time around because we had kept ourselves pure for one another.

In Jamaica we stayed in a cottage with a big ceiling fan and a balcony. The trade winds were blowing, and translucent blue water lapped up on shore. As we walked from our cottage to the hotel, we reached up and picked bananas from trees growing in rows along the path. We visited the waterfalls at Ocho Rios one day, and sat beneath them, the water streaming overhead and in front of us. The days flew past, and we talked the time away like long-lost friends.

For the first time in our relationship, neither of us had anything to hide from the other. We were free of the fears that had plagued us and free to be open and vulnerable with each other. We experienced first-hand what it means to be made new in Christ. Dave, in particular, experienced a new sense of honesty and genuineness . . . essential elements of a rebuilt marriage. He will describe what happened next.

The Tasks of Rebuilding

We went out on a sailboat one day while we were in Jamaica. Now, I'd sailed before, but not very often and only in calm waters. We left the shore, and all at once the wind shifted and the waves started to swell. No matter what I did, I could not make that boat turn around and head toward shore.

"I think we're heading for Cuba," I said to Elsie. And then I said something else—something I'd never, ever been able to admit to her before: "I'm scared." That gave Elsie a very insecure feeling, but it made me feel great. Being honest with Elsie was something new, something that drew me closer to her. Out there, buffeted by the winds and sprayed by the saltwater, it was as if our relationship was being scrubbed clean and polished and refreshed. To me, it felt wonderful, even if the boat was out of control.

There are a number of ways in which the early days of our second marriage resembled that wild sailboat ride. We were communicating—and boy, did we communicate, as we fought the wind that day! We both knew that there was no escape, no easy out. Our presence together on rough seas demanded that we team up to plan and work together.

We did, and we made it back to shore drenched and exhausted. Our second marriage has made similar demands on us. We've resolved that jumping ship is simply not an option, no matter how choppy the waters become.

Our attitude about marriage and one another has been totally different the second time around. Often, we would say to one another, "This is it. If things go wrong, we've got to work them out." We made a mutual commitment to commitment, as well as to one another. And the fact that both of us had committed our lives to Christ formed a new foundation for our relationship.

The first marriage was so typical. We had stars in our eyes, and we walked down the aisle believing that we would be happy forever. That marriage became a disaster. Marrying the same person a second time struck raw terror in my heart. All the way down the aisle I asked myself, "What in the world am I doing? How do I face family and friends if we blow it again?" I knew the pitfalls the second time. The first time, I had blinders on. The second marriage started out scary, but it has been getting better ever since.

Spiritual Tools for Rebuilding

Learning how to abide in Christ made our marriage work and gave us the tools we needed to begin the formidable task of rebuilding a shattered relationship. We prayed together, studied the Bible together and remained active at St. Stephen's. I became a lay reader and chalice bearer, a person who assists with communion and occasionally reads a lesson from the Bible during a worship service. I'll never forget the first time I helped at the communion rail, wearing white robes like the other lay readers.

I was quite preoccupied with my tasks, yet at one point I looked up at the congregation. There was Elsie, sitting near the front. She was crying. I was puzzled for a moment, and then it struck me. Looking at her was like holding up a mirror on my life, and seeing in an instant the incredible contrast between the old, drunken, know-it-all Dave, and the new, churchgoing, sober me.

I want to make it clear that the changes were not due to willpower or AA or the power of human love. A favored theme in contemporary movies and music today suggests human emotion ("love") conquers adversity and redeems our lives. That has not been our experience. Let me explain how things are different for those who abide in Christ.

Paul's letter to the Galatians lists the fruit of the Spirit: "love, joy, peace, patience, kindness, goodness, faithfulness, gentleness and self-control" (Gal 5:22-23). When Elsie and I independently received Christ as our Lord and Savior, those spiritual fruits became operative in our lives. They are totally opposed to what Paul terms "the sinful nature," the traits that had characterized our first marriage. In Christ we found forgiveness for ourselves. Then we discovered we could forgive one another (Elsie did the lion's share of the forgiving in our case). We could approach everything in a fresh way, and we could refer laughingly to my pre-Christian days. It was almost as if that pre-Christian person had never existed at all. So Elsie didn't have to seethe with anger at her first husband. And I didn't have to resent my first wife or be tempted to bluff about how I felt.

A recovering alcoholic needs to learn to live with the fact

that all along the way he will encounter reminders of the depth of his sin. A damaged relationship with a child may take a long time to heal, as we will explore in the next chapter. Learning to feel forgiven, particularly within a marriage, is crucial. Without it, there can be no "sanctuary" within the marriage.

I believe Elsie was able to freely forgive me because of the Holy Spirit's presence in her life. Ultimately, sanctuary is with God. Without his forgiveness in our lives, we cannot truly forgive one another; at best we can try to overlook a grievance.

In many ways this is the spiritual equivalent of the all-important concept of "detachment" mentioned in chapter three. When we become Christians, we die to ourselves. Our own agenda and defenses no longer monopolize who we are and what we do. To put it in biblical terms, when we know the truth, the truth sets us free. And being in Christ means we let go of codependent baggage; we seek God's will, not our own. We seek the best for ourselves and our spouses, not revenge or a redress of past wrongs.

Frequently when I counsel married couples coping with alcoholism, they ask me this question: "If I keep remembering the bad times and thinking about them, does it mean I'm not forgiven?"

I tell them that forgiveness is like scar tissue. When I was in boarding school, I had to spend many Saturday mornings raking leaves as a punishment for misbehavior. I was not at all happy about it. Once as I raked furiously, muttering about the unfairness of it all, I accidentally snagged a broken Coke bottle. It sliced right into my ankle, nicking the artery. Blood spurted everywhere, and I had to be rushed to the emergency room. When it healed, there was (and still is) a visible ridge of scar tissue there. It doesn't bleed anymore, and it doesn't hurt, but it does remind me of what happened. And now I'm very careful when I rake leaves.

It's the same with forgiven sin. After it cuts us, injures us, God heals the hurt. But he leaves the memory as a reminder: "Go and sin no more." We're meant to learn from our sin so that we do not go on hurting ourselves and others.

As Elsie and I sought to practice the presence of God in our lives, we found a way to remind ourselves daily of the spiritual commitment we had made. Through John Guest's ministry, we had learned that it was critically important to pray sincerely. That meant turning over to God the matters about which we prayed and not continuing to chew on them anxiously. For us it meant a conscious decision not to be plagued by the "what if's?" or the uncertainties of the future.

To act out the principle of turning prayers over to God, we took a paper bag, wrote "God" on it, and taped it up high on the back of our kitchen door. As I prayed about matters such as my career, my role as a father, my abilities to be a good husband, I would write down each concern on a piece of paper. Then those pieces of paper would go in the bag. The rule was that if you start worrying about a matter of prayer that you've turned over to God, you have to climb up on a chair and fish it out of the bag. I don't want to admit how much time I spent sifting through those scraps of paper. It was effective, because it made me see what was happening spiritually.

Coming into a relationship with Christ does not automatically calm the waters in a troubled marriage or any other situation. Being a Christian certainly does not prevent temporary alienation from God, or from one another, and it does not free us from disobedience. It does provide the way and means for restoration and reconciliation to occur, no matter how many times a person messes up.

Areas of Discord

In our second marriage, there were (and still are) times when insignificant or accidental occurrences trigger old feelings and behaviors. Not too long after the second wedding, Elsie accidentally locked me out of the house one day. To most people, being locked out is a temporary annoyance. For me, that bolted door triggered a flood of unpleasant memories. As I twisted the doorknob and tugged at the door, all the old feelings of anger, helplessness and self-pity surged back.

Once at our old Michigan farmhouse, Elsie locked me out when I did not come home one night. It's no wonder; she was concerned about the two little boys and wanted to get some sleep herself. I came home that night and launched into a real drunken rage. I tore the door off its hinges. The next day, suffering from a mammoth hangover, I fixed it. Locked doors still set me off for some reason, and this particular lock-out after our remarriage really annoyed me. In fact, I was furious.

Elsie heard me pounding and shouting, and she came running to get the door unlocked. What a contrast to the old days! Elsie, my first wife, would have tended to react in ways typical of a codependent spouse. She would have been fearful, apologetic, wringing her hands and promising it won't happen again. The new Elsie—my second wife—did nothing of the kind. After the door was open and I was inside, feeling a bit sheepish about my outburst, she matter-of-factly told me it was an accident. I cooled down immediately, whereas the old Dave would have stormed back out the door and down to the local tavern. We were able to talk about the incident without rancor, and we openly discussed ways in which the wake of alcoholism continued to rock our boat.

Beyond isolated incidents, there was one major area of discord which surfaced early in our second marriage. It involved my job, which kept me away from home Monday through Friday. As the first year of our second marriage wore on, Elsie began feeling more and more resentful, irritated and bitter. I could hear it in her voice when I got ready to leave each Sunday evening.

"Dave," she asked one time, "do you think you'll ever look for another job?" I certainly wasn't placing Elsie's feelings first when I responded, "I may do this for another fourteen or fifteen years."

I didn't like leaving my family behind, but wherever I went, I quickly got in touch with an AA group. It was encouraging to see active chapters all up and down the East Coast, and to get to know others who understood just what recovery is all about. Elsie, meanwhile, found herself reliving her days as a divorced single parent. It didn't help when little Hector asked all week long, "Where's Daddy?" And I began to see how my homecomings on Friday night upset the apple cart. All the week's routines were suddenly disrupted— bedtimes, mealtimes, what's permitted and what's not. I didn't know all the day-to-day rules of the house, so I broke them right and left without any regard for Elsie.

Eventually, it became harder and harder for me to get on that airplane each week. The whole point of being reconciled and remarried was to have a relationship, to spend time together. Gradually, I saw how I was damaging the very core of our commitment to one another. I wanted to be at home and engaged in the lives of my sons. I didn't want a succession of weekend, fly-by-night flings with my wife. At the same time, I enjoyed the prestige, power and economic benefits of my job.

Finally, one evening at the airport, it took a superhuman effort to get myself to put one foot in front of the other and walk up the ramp into a plane. "This has got to stop," I told myself.

What next? The alcoholic in me would have been terrified by the prospect of no employment, and it might have triggered a drinking bout.

Instead, I found myself surrounded and protected by some fellow believers who had been praying about my professional endeavors. These friends consisted of a group of guys who met to discuss the concept of a new company based on Christian principles. What would such a company look like? we wondered. How would it be managed? How would it differ from secular organizations?

Our strategy sessions gave way to planning and implementing a new company called Covenant Community Services. It specialized in doing home repair jobs that were too small for commercial contractors and too large for most homeowners to tackle by themselves. At one meeting, I critiqued the plan from my standpoint as a management consultant. A crafty friend of mine, Frank Melnick, jumped right in with a suggestion: "Why don't you come on board and run this company?" That was just the "out" I needed from my management consultant position. I gave two weeks' notice at the old job, and then I came home. Elsie will explain how she felt about that.

Maintaining a Marriage

The joy I felt at having an ordinary husband-and-wife routine at home is almost inexpressible. I knew with certainty that Dave would come home on time each evening, would stay home and play with the boys and would not need me to call his boss in the morning to say he's sick. A full seven years had passed since our first wedding, and only now did I feel as if I had a marriage. I was determined to make it work ... and work well.

I remained active in all the women's ministries St. Stephen's had to offer; looking back now at the notebooks I filled as I studied the Bible, it's as if I had enrolled in a master's degree program. I was definitely majoring in marriage. Something I heard from a speaker during this time made a deep impression on me, and his advice is particularly apt for the spouses of alcoholics.

Working from the writings of Walter Trobisch, the speaker dwelled on the topic of "Living with Unfulfilled Desires." If you are married to an alcoholic, I believe you struggle more with unfulfilled desires than sober couples can imagine. The level of companionship in your marriage may be abysmal, not even approaching a bare minimum of togetherness. Dinner out, just the two of you? A quiet evening watching television side by side? In a marriage held hostage by alcoholism it just never happens. Yet this speaker wasn't focusing on changing the heart, or even the behavior, of the difficult spouse. Instead, he encouraged spouses in tough circumstances to love and accept *themselves.* "You cannot change your partner," he pointed out. "You can change yourself."

Unfulfilled desires are an inescapable reality of life,

I learned, and they should not keep us from living an abundant, joy-filled life. Percolating just beneath the surface of most good marriages untouched by alcoholism are plenty of unfulfilled desires: a nicer home, a second child, a better job, a cross-country move. Spouses of alcoholics need to remind themselves often that the absence of alcohol will not, by itself, eliminate problems from their marriages.

As I listened to this helpful speaker, I couldn't help but flash back to the days of our first marriage and the crushing loneliness I felt. What I was hearing addressed the very core of the pain and confusion I had felt as our marriage fell apart. It gave me a completely new way of understanding myself, as well as the tools I needed to maintain a strong, lasting marriage.

I knew I still had a long way to go. I could readily see how Dave had changed, but some aspects of my attitude toward him hadn't caught up completely. I found it difficult, at times, to express anger or other negative emotions to him, and I struggled with our sexual relationship. It helped to see what the Bible had to say: "The wife's body does not belong to her alone but also to her husband. In the same way, the husband's body does not belong to him alone but also to his wife" (1 Cor 7:4). And the study groups and retreats I attended at St. Stephen's addressed the toughest issues without flinching.

I keep returning, even now, to a list I made then. I believe it contains practical wisdom for any believer struggling in a marriage where one spouse is a recovering alcoholic:

1. Pray for your spouse every day.
2. Think of, and thank God for, the gifts and attributes he

has given your husband or wife.

3. Make your sexual relationship a priority, not an afterthought.

4. Keep your relationship to the Lord growing, regardless of what your spouse does. Ask God to fill you with love for your husband or wife.

5. Don't let resentments pile up. Ask forgiveness and share problems. Express them this way: "I feel angry when _____ happens."

6. Work and play together often.

All my study and prayer and fellowship were working wonders in my life. Soon, however, my avid pursuit of spiritual opportunities began to throw our relationship off balance. Dave developed a tendency to defer to me on any subject having to do with church or Bible study, because intellectually I knew more than he did. This is not unusual, even in marriages where alcoholism is not a factor. When it is a factor, all the old struggles with low self-esteem may continue to surface. A significant difference between my first husband and the new Dave soon became apparent. The new Dave was willing to work hard to change the things he didn't like about himself, his job and our relationship. For the first time, I could really begin to believe that problems had solutions. Dave no longer became intractably mired in self-pity, seeking escape rather than answers.

I'll let him explain what helped then and what has continued to keep our marriage whole and thriving.

Staying on Track

I don't believe God predestined or "willed" me to be an alcoholic, and I do not believe he intended for us to get divorced. The two of us did those things by ourselves. But after we messed up our lives, we repented and returned to the Lord. Then we began to see how God could bring good out of bad.

I view the circumstances of my conversion as a prime example of what I call the thick-skull theory of divine intervention. The best illustration I've heard of this theory involves a story of two farmers and one mule. The first farmer tells the second, "This mule will do whatever you want him to do. Just tell him what you want." So the second farmer tells the mule: "Plow that field!" The mule stands motionless. "Plow that field!" shouts the second farmer, raising his voice. The mule doesn't move. Finally, the second farmer calls the first farmer back over to his field. "This mule won't do a thing I ask him to," he says. Then the first one brandishes a baseball bat and smacks the mule right between the eyes. "Plow that field," says the first farmer. The mule obediently begins plowing, row after row. "You needed to get his attention," says the first farmer.

Sometimes it's no easy matter for God to get our attention. How many smacks between the eyes does it take?

Staying active in AA and taking other steps to keep my recovery on track does not contradict the certainty we feel about God's role in all this. He did work miracles in our lives and marriage, and we are new creations in him, as Elsie has written. At the same time, the process of recovery requires people such as me to stick with a course of action. And being around other alcoholics not only benefits me. I have learned that my participation was a blessing and an encouragement to others as well. Helping others by remaining active is a bedrock principle of AA. And church is no substitute for the companionship of fellow recovering alcoholics.

Those were extremely busy days for me. I was directing the business affairs of a new company, trying my best to be a good father to two young boys, participating in church activities and scheduling time to spend with Elsie. It was tempting at times to skip those twice-weekly AA meetings. Yet I knew, and I had been told by John L., that it was essential for me to keep showing up.

Each week, I would attend one open and one closed meeting. The open meetings are large, coffee-and-fellowship gatherings at which one person generally tells his or her story. Attending the open meetings is a way for an alcoholic to maintain a sense of identity.

In the rush of commitments and activities I did not often stop to reflect on the fact that I was always one drink away from slipping right back into the depths of alcohol-induced self-destruction. Going to the AA meetings faithfully reminded me of that inescapable truth and helped keep me on an even emotional keel.

The closed meetings, as I've mentioned before, concentrate on small-group discussion. It is in that context that alcoholics grow and develop close relationships with one another. They stay accountable, and they fine-tune the challenging details of living day-to-day in a society where alcohol, and seductive messages about it, are ever-present.

I am certain that I would not have remained sober if I had stopped going to meetings. Even today, I have to guard against extremes and keep myself from getting too tired or too hungry. Anything that would send me out of whack emotionally has to be avoided; and AA helps people recognize those triggers and cope with them.

Rotten Apples

Professionally, something very strange began happening in my life. I sensed an insistent call from God to enter full-time ministry. I wondered how in the world God could use me. I simply couldn't understand it, as my low sense of self-worth emerged. If God wants someone to be really effective, then why doesn't he call someone who has his act together? Someone with a lot of ability and many resources would surely perform better than me.

My insecurities were all too typical of recovering alcoholics, no matter what their profession or calling. Just as they need to rebuild relationships, and particularly their marriages, they also need to rebuild self-confidence through the encouragement of others who understand them.

In my case a very gifted Australian clergyman named Alf Stanway came to Sewickley. When I talked with him about my sense of being drawn toward ministry and my overpowering sense of inadequacy due to my alcoholism, he had a ready answer. He said, "You think God has reached into the apple barrel and pulled out a rotten one. You don't realize all the other apples are rotten too. You know you're rotten; some of the others don't recognize their own condition yet." Then he cited a parable and a question Jesus asked which put my circumstances in perspective.

"Two men owed money to a certain moneylender. One owed him five hundred denarii, and the other fifty. Neither of them had the money to pay him back, so he canceled the debts of both. Now which of them will love him more?" Jesus asked. (Lk 7:41-42)

The answer is clear: the one whose debt was greater.

Alf Stanway explained to me that the Christian who has

been forgiven greatly is God's most effective worker. "And besides," he told me, "you're the best he's got." I can remember thinking, "If I'm the best God's got, then God is in real trouble." Yet after more than a decade in ministry, I am more convinced than ever that our perspective is skewed. We tend to look at one another and see vast differences. God looks down and sees us all falling short.

Soon after that, I began reading for orders (preparing to enter seminary). In September 1976, I entered Trinity Episcopal School for Ministry. I had no idea what God had in store for me, but I was committed to a ministry of counsel and healing for families plagued by alcoholism. Like all the clergy at St. Stephen's, I wanted to see marriages flourish, and most of all for individuals—whatever their position in life—to come to a saving knowledge of Jesus Christ.

Learning to Be a Dad

At home, meanwhile, life had taken an unexpected and radical twist. Elsie and I had discussed the possibility of having another child, even though it was unlikely she would conceive again. We didn't give the matter much thought until one day, Elsie announced she was pregnant. She was due to deliver in January 1975.

Toward the very end of Elsie's pregnancy, she learned during a check-up that we were expecting twins. She arrived home just as I got back from picking Davie up after kindergarten, and she burst into tears and blurted out the news. I responded by walking into a wall.

Two weeks later, our six-pound baby girls, Rosanna and Margaret, were born. That event helped me see Elsie in a whole new light. After giving birth, she came down with the flu. She was extremely weak and sick and remained in the hospital for ten days. It terrified me to see her hooked up to IVs with her face and lips a sickly shade of blue. "Lord, you know me and you know how much I need Elsie," I prayed. "You cannot take her away now!" Finally she and the girls came home. I was able to take a substantial amount of time off from work, so for the first time in my life I was fully engaged in taking care of my young children. The management consultant in me emerged before long. I made a chart showing when each of the girls ate, slept and had a diaper change. When one of them cried, I checked the chart to see which one was due for what.

Experiencing a double dose of full-time infant care gave me a profound appreciation for what Elsie went through when Hector and Davie were little. I had been so wrapped up in myself and my drinking that I scarcely noticed what they did or what they needed. And as Elsie recuperated, I would see her watching me with a look of stunned surprise on her face. It looked as if she was thinking, "Could this really be Dave MacKenzie . . . the same guy who had insisted that real men, especially Marines, don't change diapers?"

When I was drinking, it never occurred to me that I should cultivate parenting skills. I was no more equipped to be a father than to quarterback the Superbowl. The memories of how I treated Hector and Davie during those early years still hurt. One of my most difficult moments came about when we were divorced. Hector was a preschooler, deeply troubled by my absence and Elsie's obvious distress. One day after one of my earliest visits with the boys, Hector let us know exactly how he felt, without saying a word. . . .

CHAPTER 7

The Alcoholic Parent

*I*t was a typical Sunday afternoon visit with the boys at *Dave's parents' home, not long after the divorce. After Elsie dropped the boys off, Dave held Davie on his lap and watched three-year-old Hector roll down the hill in the front yard. He laughed with abandon each time as he picked up speed, and he came bounding back up the hill tirelessly. The boys' grandmother took Davie inside to play with a big box of toys she kept on hand. Hector begged for a ride on Dave's motorcycle, so Dave seated the tot carefully in front of him and took a spin around the block.*

The two-hour visit flew past, and Elsie's car reappeared in the driveway. Dave walked outside with both boys, and handed Davie to Elsie. When Dave opened the car door for Hector, he didn't say a word. He began pushing and tugging at his dad, trying desperately to get him inside the car. Dave's throat constricted, and he felt physically wounded by the message little Hector was trying to send. Dave stood there stonefaced, not daring to show any emotion.

Finally, Dave had to peel Hector's hands off his leg and forcibly place him inside the car. Gritting his teeth to hold back tears, Dave marched into the house; then he broke down and cried bitterly. Here was an innocent three-year-old child who had no say whatsoever about what was happening to him. He was signaling in the most eloquent way possible that he wanted and needed his daddy back. He was hurting terribly, and some of the insecurities that developed in him during that period of divorce are still with him today.

A few months later, Hector got suspended from nursery school for three days because he bit another child. On the day Elsie picked him up after the biting incident, his teacher marched out to the car and stuck her head in the window. "You have got to get that boy a father!" she told Elsie. Elsie kept her silence, but she fumed inwardly, "If you only knew what his father was like. . . ."

The Young Child
In many ways, we were fortunate. In our family, a blow-up over alcoholism occurred very early on. At the time of our remarriage, Hector was five years old and Davie was three. They certainly suffered some consequences of spending their infancies in an imbalanced family setting. Nonetheless, they did not have to endure having an actively alcoholic parent for years on end. In many cases that is what happens. The effects on the children are profound.

It is not just the behavior of the alcoholic parent that poses problems for the children, although that is certainly a prime source of difficulty. As we have noted throughout this book, the effects of alcoholism touch every member of a family, impacting most directly on the spouse. The children, as a result, not only have to cope with an alcoholic parent who is unpredictable, often absent and frequently abusive; they also have to learn to relate to a nonalcoholic parent who may be codependent and who is likely to be so wrapped up in coping with the alcoholism that he or she cannot adequately and consistently meet the needs of the children.

It has often been noted that children in alcoholic homes do not know what a normal childhood is like. They live daily with uncertainty, fear, denial and guilt. The significant adults in their lives tiptoe around the elephant in the living room, preoccupied with the mess but never naming the source (or cleaning it up). So the children imitate their parents. According to counseling expert Dr. Charlene Hoar, these children "learn three rules of survival: don't talk, don't trust and don't let yourself feel anything."[1]

Why do children raised in a setting permeated by alcohol need survival tactics such as these? Dave's family was typical: growing up with an alcoholic mother, the children never knew exactly what to expect. He learned early on, however, that it was a bad idea to make Mom mad. He explains how his upbringing was affected by his mother's alcoholism, and how those experiences shaped his approach to child rearing.

A Childhood Endured (Not Enjoyed)
"Mama Khrushchev" is what we called my mother behind

her back, because she had a temper and ruled with an iron fist. If I brought home a bad report card, I was terrified to show it to her; she never hit, but her yelling and verbal abuse hurt far worse than a spanking. If I brought home a good report card, I felt disappointed. Mom would see five As and a B, yet her response was to ask "What's that B doing there?" Alcohol greatly exaggerated a critical spirit in her.

Her unpredictable and inconsistent parenting had an impact on a daily basis, not just occasionally. I can vividly recall my mother watching benignly as I scattered toys around the living room. The next day when I embarked on the very same task, she would scream and threaten. Her response to her children depended on whether (and how much) she was drinking, not on defined limits or household rules that were clearly communicated.

After Mom died in 1988, my brothers and sister and I began to compare notes about our childhoods. None of the stories agreed completely; we quickly discovered that each of our perceptions of reality was different. We had always joked about how Mom embellished stories about the family after she had a few drinks. Her tales were never the same, and we never could sort out what was true and what was not. As we grew up, we learned that this affected us in terms of how we perceived ourselves and how we discerned what is "true."

Melissa, my sister, told me I had always seemed like such a happy child; yet I don't remember a happy childhood. I remember a childhood marked by tension, anxiety and a desperate seeking of acceptance. Childhood was something endured rather than enjoyed.

In my home what happened was very typical of the alcoholic home. Mom kept her drinking hidden. She denied she was drinking, but the unmistakable effects were obvious. It is easy for the alcoholic parent to keep on denying the problem, because children want so badly to trust and believe the parent that they will buy whatever story is told. The result is an elaborate coverup, a household tense with anger and stark inconsistencies in how children are treated from day to day.

It is not difficult to imagine the consequences of alcoholism on matters of parenting. An alcoholic father may be a model parent when he is sober (particularly if he feels guilty about drinking). He may promise the child a special weekend outing: "Let's go pick out a new bike for you on Saturday." Then when Saturday arrives, the father goes on a drinking binge. Suddenly, he is surly, short-tempered and incoherent. The child may try to remind Dad about the promised trip to the bike shop, only to be flatly rejected.

Enter the mother who tries to comfort the child by obscuring the truth. "Dad's been under so much pressure at work," she'll say. "Why don't you just leave him alone this weekend?" As scenes such as this play out over weeks and months and years, there are a number of predictable results:

☐ The child loses any sense of what is true and what is not.

☐ Confusion sets in as the child seeks to be like the parent.

☐ The child might cry out for help or attention in very inappropriate ways or withdraw.

☐ Self-esteem plummets, because the child receives such mixed messages from the parents.

☐ The child loses friends or stops trying to make friends, because it is so painful and embarrassing to bring a classmate home not knowing what shape the alcoholic parent will be in.

☐ Feelings of guilt emerge; the child feels responsible for the parent's condition, and the alcoholic parent may even tell the child, "You drive me to drink."

Counselor Janet Geringer Woititz, in her book *Marriage on the Rocks,* summarizes the effects of alcoholism on children this way:

> The child from the alcoholic home does not see himself as capable. If he was [sic] truly capable, he would be able to figure out a way to get his father to stop drinking. Everything else pales by comparison. He dismisses anything that he does as unimportant. What difference does it make if he can build something, or can get A's in math, if his father is drunk all the time and his mother is preoccupied and nobody really cares?[2]

Breaking the Cycle

Children are resilient, and they respond remarkably well to positive changes in the family no matter how bad life has become. Even before the alcoholic spouse begins to recover, the other spouse can make a difference in how the child views himself and his circumstances. First, the non-alcoholic parent needs to be honest and forthright, explaining the disease of alcoholism in terms appropriate for the child's age and ability to understand.

Coming clean about the problem accomplishes several things: it restores honesty to the home, and it relieves guilt. Children may need to be told explicitly, "This is not your fault." As it happened, there was an aching need for us to do this with our sons. It had never occurred to us, until one evening when Elsie was tucking the boys into bed several months after the remarriage.

She had been reading extensively about marital and family relations, and all her reading prompted her to say casually, "You know, all the bad things that happened are not your fault." She expected them to respond indifferently, if at all, but that was not the case. Hector, in particular, sat upright in bed. "Really, Mommy?" he asked, searching her face. Elsie sat down beside him. "Absolutely not," she said. "It was Daddy's illness that made us get so angry with each other. Now that's behind us. It's okay now." We had no reason to suspect they were harboring anxious feelings about the past, yet clearly they were.

Along with a new policy of openness in the home, the non-alcoholic spouse can help by acknowledging the feelings of the child and encouraging their expression. Saying "I know you are worried about your dad" may elicit some sorely needed sharing of emotions.

Finally, just as there is AA for the alcoholic and Al-Anon for the spouse, there are groups known as Alateen and Alatot for children. They operate (very successfully) under the same principles as Al-Anon. At an Alateen meeting, the child of an alcoholic may for the first time meet others who have lived through the same confusion and pain. Often, to simply hear the words "I know what you mean because it happened to me" is to begin to heal emotionally.

Family Fears, Family Decisions

When an alcoholic parent makes a commitment to recovery, parenting takes on some new challenges beyond restoring hurt relationships. Breaking the cycle means discussing alcoholism clearly and often, and it means establishing a family decision about whether all should abstain from alcohol or whether (if they are not alcoholics) family members may choose to drink moderately. Perhaps the most daunting challenge is this: parenting for a recovering alcoholic means educating your children effectively so they stay alert for signs of alcoholism in their own lives.

This is crucial, because there appears to be a strong inherited tendency toward alcoholism. Studies have shown consistently that approximately twenty-four per cent of the children of one alcoholic parent may become alcoholics as well. When both parents are alcoholic, the percentage jumps to around sixty-four per cent. So, in our case the chances are good that one of our children could become an alcoholic. Elsie and I had wondered what that would be like. One night, I had the chance to take an unexpected look. Hector was seventeen, and he had gone out with a friend on a Friday night. He and his buddy polished off an entire bottle of whiskey in less than an hour. Then they went to a party. The alcohol took hold, and Hector's legs began buckling under him. "Call my dad," he mumbled. His friends called home and told me Hector was having "car trouble." I didn't think much of it, and told them to call back if he couldn't get the engine started in another half-hour or so. Hector sent his friends straight back to the telephone. "Tell Dad I'm bombed," he insisted.

They called back in ten minutes and told the truth. Meanwhile, Hector had collapsed and was unconscious. When I reached the party, Hector's friends had him propped up. His eyes were open, but he had virtually no muscle control at all. I carried him out to the car, not saying a word. Seeing him this way was profoundly jarring. It was as if I were being forced to watch a videotape of myself from my college days.

The alcoholic believes the lie of alcohol. Once the effect takes hold, the drinker believes all his or her social skills are enhanced. A sense of being supremely witty, attractive and sparkling sets in.

Yet the reality of drunkenness is so very different from the alcohol-induced fantasy. Certainly, Hector did not feel witty or sparkling as he groaned in the front seat of the car, but what compelled him to drink in the first place was the belief that alcohol would do good things for him. Seeing how it truly affects a person drove home to me in indisputable eloquence just how I had looked to Elsie. It was grotesque and humiliating.

The motion of the car began affecting Hector, and he hung his head out the window, retching. I had said almost nothing to him, apart from a warning: "Don't puke in my car."

The incident was so unsettling that Elsie and I never did become angry with Hector, who fully anticipated being grounded forever. After cleaning him up and putting him in bed, I knelt down next to the bed and prayed for him for a long time. The morning after, Hector dragged himself outdoors and began mowing the grass, a Saturday chore he'd promised to do. He was clearly shaken by the events of the night before. No additional discipline was required.

The point here is twofold: Hector learned a lesson about alcohol the hard way, but he also had learned well before his binge that he could trust his dad; he knew how well I understood. From the time he was in junior high school, we had been teaching him about alcohol: spelling out the realities of what it can do to a person; listing the signs of alcoholism and how to recognize them; and generally trying to remove the mystique and the appeal liquor holds for young boys (and girls). A couple days after the incident, I sat down with Hector and talked about what had happened. I reviewed the tell-tale signs of alcoholism with him and told him to watch for them in his friends. "They need to know about this," I told him, "even if it ticks them off."

If people can't make a decision to stop drinking, if they exhibit mood or personality changes, if it appears they have to get drunk every time they drink . . . those are the warning signals of alcoholism. Hector, as well as Davie and the twins, have had this drummed into them frequently. Hector, in particular, is very aware of it and very cautious about drinking. On some occasions, he has told his friends that he's choosing not to drink because "my dad's an alcoholic, and I have a twenty-four per cent chance of becoming one myself."

Hector is an adult now and a college graduate. He does drink socially, and he even worked as a bartender for two years. He does not, however, drink irresponsibly. He is not an alcoholic because he remains fully in control of how much and how often he imbibes.

Teaching children about alcohol and about personal responsibility is one important way to break the cycle of abuse. It must begin with a decision by you and your spouse. If you are a recovering alcoholic, then drinking is never an option for you. Your spouse may wisely choose to abstain as well, because of personal conviction or a sense of solidarity with the recovering alcoholic.

In this case you probably will not serve alcohol in your home or order drinks when you go out. For many families in which there is a recovering alcoholic, and for many Christian families in general, abstinence is a favored choice. Avoiding alcohol—and other mood-altering chemicals—is consistent with a biblical understanding of our bodies as temples of the Holy Spirit.

For reasons of physical health as well as spiritual well-being, abstinence makes sense. Increasingly, the ill effects of alcohol are being recognized—even in those who drink in moderation. Alcohol impairs unborn children, it endangers motorists, it contributes to a host of chronic illnesses and it is not consistent with society's emphasis on nutrition and exercise. As a result, fewer people are drinking. Breweries are even marketing several varieties of nonalcoholic "beer" to appeal to a changing social consensus.

At the same time, alcohol is not yet an endangered species of beverage. In homes that have not been touched by alcoholism, and where alcohol is served or consumed responsibly, we believe young people have a built-in opportunity to learn a responsible approach to alcohol. Elsie grew up in a home where wine with dinner was the norm, and before-dinner cocktails appeared occasionally, particularly if guests were there.

In her home the focus was on social interaction. Alcohol was incidental to the main event, whether it was a family dinner or a party. In my home alcohol was central, and social occasions revolved around it.

Even when you choose abstinence, education about alcohol is crucial, as well as discussions about drug abuse and addiction in general. Your children will be confronted with plenty of opportunities and invitations to drink when they are away from home, even when they are surprisingly young.

When the Child Grows Up
In this chapter, we have outlined several experiences that

children of alcoholics tend to share in common. These experiences frequently result in personality traits which linger into adulthood, contributing to a phenomenon that has become known as Adult Children of Alcoholics (ACOA).

An apt summary of what ACOAs feel and how they behave appeared in an article in *Christianity Today* by author Charles Sell:

Sensing the feverish panic of life out of control, (children of alcoholics) use vast amounts of energy and effort to stabilize their lives. Each develops his or her own method of coping, some withdrawing, others rebelling. Some . . . take the place of the irresponsible parent and act as parents at a time when they need to be parented. Because they become so accustomed to pacifying the alcoholic parent, many turn into placaters, always avoiding conflict and wanting to please.

Carried over into adulthood, these survival tactics can create many problems. Withdrawers may turn into lonely adults who are unable to relate and be intimate with others. Rescuers can end up being addicted to people who need them; they burn themselves out helping others, often feeling like victims and feeling angry because they cannot say no. . . . They frequently marry alcoholics. Placaters feel at fault for all the bad around them and are filled with guilt and self-loathing.[3]

The number of adult children of alcoholics in the United States may be as high as 22 million, or thirteen per cent of the population. Across the country, support groups for ACOAs have been forming now for several years. In some cases these groups emerge from church ministries to chemically dependent people and their families; others are community-based. Local chapters of AA, Al-Anon, Alateen or community mental health centers can provide referrals.

Perhaps you are coping with ACOA difficulties as well as alcoholism in your marriage. That would not be surprising, since alcoholism appears to be passed from one generation to the next as it was in my family. The inconsistencies and mood swings exhibited by my mom did not diminish over time. I believe they contributed to some of the difficulties I have faced as a parent.

A Legacy of Rejection

Right up until my mother died, my relationship with her was uncomfortable and distant. Just about every aspect of how we interacted with her was colored by her drinking. In 1988 we planned a family vacation into Canada. We scheduled a stop in Pittsburgh to see Mom on our way north.

When she wasn't drinking, Mom was a terrific person and a warm-hearted grandmother. Hector remembers her as "a great lady," someone he loved to visit. The kids, especially when they were little, would innocently ask questions about Nana's drinking and her erratic behavior. Rosie would see the glass of vodka Nana carried with her constantly, and ask for a sip. Nana would reply, "This is for my cough. Go get your own water." Hector, who was old enough to understand what was going on, asked about it one time. I told him not to get mixed up in it; just be her grandson, I told him, and let her be your Nana.

When your parent is an alcoholic, however, nothing is simple. We couldn't just show up whenever we rolled into Sewickley and knock on her door. I knew we would have to plan to see her in the morning, before her drinking got out of hand later in the day. So when we reached Pittsburgh on the first day of our vacation, we checked into a motel, and I called Mom. "Hi, we're in town," I told her. "I just called to confirm that we'll be over to see you tomorrow morning." She was drunk, and here is what she said in response: "Don't come. I'm very busy; I don't want to see you."

No matter how much perspective I had gained concerning alcoholism and ACOA traits, Mom's chilly rejection still hurt. A parent always wields emotional power over a child, power even to put an over-forty-year-old child back into a six-year-old frame of mind. The alcoholic parent often does this deliberately to manipulate circumstances or to generate sympathy.

I suspected Mom would be less than enthusiastic about our visit, and I was able to chalk it up to the effects of the alcohol. So I said, "Well, we're going to show up tomorrow morning. I hope you'll see us." And of course, as certainly as day follows night, she was all smiles and hugs for the grandkids the next day.

Having grown up with inconsistency and rejection at home, I am typical of adult children of alcoholics: I have difficulty relating normally to people because early models of normal interactions were absent. For me, these difficulties can erupt very suddenly in displays of temper . . . and, unfortunately, my children are often the unwitting targets.

Shortly after our remarriage, my temper got away from me over an incident that should have caused no stir at all. We were in Florida, relaxing on the beach. Davie, who was about five years old, splashed some water on me. I blew my stack and began chasing him. When I caught him, I pushed him down. Afterwards, I felt terribly guilty. He was so little and energetic, and he was just trying to engage me in play. I didn't say anything about it for years, and then in 1988 I brought it up. I wanted to apologize, even though I figured he had completely forgotten about it. I was wrong. He remembered it vividly. Now I wonder how many times Davie avoided me because he was afraid of the consequences.

Hector recalls a temperamental dad from those early days of the remarriage, particularly during the year in which I was on the road every Monday through Friday. "The last thing we wanted to do was to make you mad," he's told me. On Saturday mornings, he and Davie learned to sit quietly and watch cartoons on television rather than try to play with me.

The boys clearly exhibited some of the defense tactics referred to earlier. They didn't talk, they grew wary of me, and they kept their feelings concealed for fear of the consequences. As you or your spouse recover from alcoholism, it may be essential for you to take a hard look at what you are doing as a parent. Are some of the old behavior patterns (such as inconsistency or temper flare-ups) still evident? You can take the initiative now to minimize the ACOA difficulties your children may one day face.

Parenting and Faith

A poor or chaotic relationship with a parent, particularly a father, can impede a person's ability to trust God and relate to him as a Heavenly Father. This is certainly true for ACOAs, who may be inclined to repeat as adults some of the behaviors they learned as children from alcoholic homes. They may go overboard in seeking approval, unable to comprehend or accept God's unconditional love.

They may feel incapable of restoring normal relationships within their family or find it extremely difficult to communicate effectively with a spouse. We have good news for them: God can make a difference; he can restore wholeness to those who may feel it has always remained just out of reach. God is interested in sustaining our relationships with him and with one another; he wants to see us all "go the distance" in our lives and (for those who marry) with our spouses.

The final chapter of this book is a reflection on "going the distance" in a marriage threatened profoundly by alcoholism. Written just after our twenty-fourth wedding anniversary, it is our attempt to explore what it takes to remain married (happily) and why it is so worthwhile to make the effort. And at times it *has* required effort. Even as recently as 1988, on our family vacation to Canada, we had a serious blow-up, right in front of the kids. Weathering that storm was nothing compared to our divorce and reconciliation, but it does indicate that the work of staying married, especially for the couple affected by alcoholism, is never finished.

CHAPTER 8

Going the Distance

*I*t was the summer of 1988, and together we left home with Davie, Rosie and Margaret for a vacation. As we meandered north in our van, heading toward St. John's, New Brunswick, Canada, a fight to end all fights broke out between us. There is no doubt about it. This was the worst altercation of our remarried life. And, as so often happens, the opening verbal shots were fired over an incredibly trivial matter.

Elsie had organized the trip, and she was in charge of planning where we would stay each night. She had not made reservations in advance, since we didn't know exactly how long we were going to stay in each spot or how far we would travel each day.

So, come evening, the search would begin for suitable

lodging. Reservations or no reservations, Elsie had a clear picture in her mind of the sort of place we should stay: a quaint New England country inn, painted white, with a grassy lawn, a cozy restaurant and a few guest rooms equipped with fluffy down comforters on each bed and fresh flowers on the dresser.

One day as dusk began to fall, Dave wheeled the van slowly through some small upstate New York town. Elsie was straining in the twilight to read the AAA travel guide, trying to make sense of a small map showing how to get to an especially quaint country inn. Dave had done the lion's share of the driving that day, so he was frazzled and worn out. Then our conversation went something like this:

Elsie, put the guide book away. There is a motel right over there. That's where we're staying.

Dave, I thought I was in charge of choosing where we would stay. Just let me tell you how to get to the inn. We're within a couple blocks of it, I'm sure.

Forget it, Elsie. What we need is a place to spend the night, not some overpriced honeymoon suite.

The chill settled in. Elsie glared out the window and tried to rein in a flood of memories of previous fights with Dave. She spoke icily. "Fine. Do whatever you want, Dave. Don't bother to listen to me."

Silence. From the back seat, an exasperated Rosie spoke up. "Mom, let's just go to the motel, OK? You and Dad are wrecking the trip. Cut it out!"

The brakes squealed as we pulled in next to the front door of an extremely average-looking motel. A neon sign blinked haphazardly. Dave spoke tersely to the girl behind the front desk, got two room keys, and hopped back in the driver's seat, slamming the door hard as he revved the engine.

We unloaded suitcases in the dark . . . grim-faced, saying nothing. Inside the rooms, instead of being greeted by down comforters and cut flowers, we found the ragged end of a cable, from which a television had been severed. The next morning, the kids decided to go for a swim. They returned to the rooms in an instant, glumly reporting that the pool had no water in it—just a layer of heavy green pond scum. Needless to say, Dave's choice of accommodations was not very popular.

We checked out the next day and continued on our way. But the fight didn't end. It became a tense standoff, settling in like a persistent sinus infection. Rosie told us—more than once—that it ruined the entire vacation for her.

What in the world happened? At a vulnerable moment, our tempers got the better of us. We found ourselves thrust back into the same emotions and behaviors we exhibited when alcohol was a constant companion and before we knew the Lord. Dave felt angry and dug in his heels. "I don't have to justify every little mistake," he groused. "And Elsie shouldn't be so touchy if things don't go exactly her way." Meanwhile, Elsie made a conscious decision to match stubbornness with stubbornness. She was not going to give in, and that was final.

Communication Breakdown

We don't recall how many weeks went by before Dave decided to apologize. We both knew we would have to deal with this eventually, and we were reminded anew of a very significant aspect of our second marriage. Because of Jesus Christ, our commitment to one another was secure. Neither of us had to worry about, or guess at, the other's sense of being permanently married.

In this episode we experienced a twofold communication breakdown. We deliberately stopped communicating with one another in order to cling to the position each of us felt was right. And we neglected to pray about it immediately, to communicate first with the Lord, whom we both acknowledged as the center of our lives and marriage.

Would our fight over hotel accommodations have erupted if our marriage had not taken its detour through divorce court? If Dave were not an alcoholic? Probably. Yet the realities of an alcoholic past and alcoholism recovery in the present color that conflict in particular ways.

If you or your spouse have weathered a course of treatment for alcoholism and you are both committed to making your marriage work, you may still meet with blow-ups similar to ours. In those circumstances it is crucial for each spouse to understand some of the obstacles and some of the advantages that exist because of alcoholism recovery.

Recovery lasts for the rest of an alcoholic's life, so gaining understanding and perspective about marital relations is essential for "going the distance." Once active alcoholism is in your past, there is every reason to believe your marriage can strive successfully toward the two primary goals outlined back in chapter one: bonding (or becoming one) and sanctuary (creating a safe and peaceful harbor for one another). As that process goes forward, there are some important factors for you to keep in mind.

To begin with, each of the factors that commonly lead to marital discord and divorce is greatly exaggerated by alcoholism. Many of them are apparent in the character traits of the alcoholic and the marital imbalance brought on by them.

Let's review some these traits, mentioned throughout this book, in order to lay a foundation for understanding how to "go the distance." When you or your spouse suffered from alcoholism, what happened?

☐ You failed to mature emotionally, because you avoided solving problems and opted to "drown your sorrows."

☐ "Distancing" set in as you spent more and more time away from home, drinking and becoming increasingly self-absorbed.

☐ Gradually, you relinquished more and more adult responsibilities to your nondrinking spouse and even your children; you became increasingly dependent and unreliable.

☐ Lying and deceit became commonplace as a way to avoid confrontation about drinking and to conceal the extent of its grip on your life. Financial problems developed for at least two reasons: because of money spent on liquor and because job stability and career advancement were sacrificed on the altar of booze.

Each of these traits of the alcoholic relates directly to some of the leading causes of a troubled marriage: money problems, poor communication, a relationship out of balance, conflicts that fester unresolved and an absence of honesty. Add to them the sheer disgust, frustration, anger and bewilderment of the spouse, and they point unmistakably in the direction of divorce court.

The couple who seeks help before their marriage explodes may clearly recognize that they must get rid of the alcohol that is at the source of all their troubles. But when that happens, the battle is far from finished. And, as we have seen, life during the early stages of recovery may be even more difficult. All the old patterns and expectations are being shattered, and the process of restoring a healthy balance to the marriage is painful, takes time and does not always move forward at a steady pace. Frequently, expectations outpace real change.

The classic AA text *Alcoholics Anonymous* says it this way:

Family confidence in Dad is rising high. The good old days will soon be back, they think. Sometimes they demand that Dad bring them back instantly! God, they believe, almost owes this recompense on a long overdue account. But the head of the house has spent years in pulling down the structures of business, romance, friendship, health—these things are now ruined or damaged. It will take time to clear away the wreck. Though old buildings will eventually be replaced by finer ones, the new structures will take years to complete.[1]

A Firm Foundation

There are times in our marriage today when some aspects of alcoholism still play out. If we become estranged in our sexual relationship, Dave feels as if he's being rejected. He continues to have mood swings that produce vexing problems, and they need to be dealt with right away. If we don't talk them out and solve the problem, that leads to a loss of intimacy between us. The longer it goes on, the more difficult and more painful it is to pull it back together again.

The main point is this: our relationship takes work, and it requires a daily affirmation and acknowledgment of the presence of God in our lives. We hold one another account-

able. If Elsie were not in the picture—or if she'd been
replaced by someone else—that would not happen nearly as
effectively as it does now. Dave says it best:

She lived through the worst of times, she knows me
thoroughly and she can pop my balloon very easily when
it needs popping.

Mile-high expectations may clash with the realities of inch-
by-inch recovery from alcoholism, as the former alcoholic
learns new habits, new social skills and new ways of relating
to people. Loss of respect in the eyes of coworkers and,
particularly, children may be difficult to recover. And a
nagging concern about people dredging up the past may
impede relationships. These are some of the obstacles you
may face as you rebuild a marriage during alcoholism
recovery. There are some advantages too. Active involve-
ment in AA and Al-Anon provides specific tools for implementing recovery. When a conflict occurs, you may fall back
on the Twelve Step program once again. It is entirely biblical,
and applicable to individuals coping with any sort of personal
or relational difficulty. Turning toward God, searching our
hearts, admitting our wrongs, making amends are integral
parts of the alcohol recovery process. Put them to use in your
marriage recovery process as well.

AA and Al-Anon provide the additional benefit of a safety
net. There is never a time of the day or night when you
cannot call for help, advice, a listening ear or a word of
empathy. And there are times when you may be called upon
as well to assist another recovering alcoholic or spouse
through a tough time. Self-esteem increases as you gain
confidence in your ability to help and be helped.

As the AA quote above suggests, "new structures" are not

built in a day. Nor can they stand on an insufficient foundation. Once, Elsie was watching a public television show called "This Old House." On this particular installment a couple in Santa Barbara had purchased a period house and were having it extravagantly remodeled. In the midst of the renovation project, workmen discovered the house had no foundation. It had been built directly on the earth beneath it. The project came to a sudden halt, and there was real fear the house would collapse. It had to be rebuilt from scratch, beginning with a solid foundation.

This image is not new to anyone familiar with the Gospels. The man who built his house on the rock met the worst of storms with confident peace-of-mind, Matthew tells us. The man whose house was built on sand, however, could not withstand even a stiff breeze.

In a Christian marriage, Christ is the foundation, and that means more than two spouses making individual commitments to Christ. It means surrendering our own wills for the marriage to Jesus.

The way in which our infamous vacation argument played out made it clear that we had moved temporarily off the foundation on which we both desired to base our marriage. In a marriage that is not honoring Christ, a time of discord means sticking up for yourself. You bump heads to determine who will "win." And in the end, both of you lose.

Since Dave's background is in management consulting, we often draw a parallel to business. In a secular marriage, it's as if the marriage partners head up two separate companies. One manufactures widgets, and the other wants to retail widgets. If they disagree—if negotiations break down over price or delivery schedules—then they just don't do business.

A difference of opinion ends in a standoff and, probably, a long look at the competition.

In a marriage where Christ is not king God does not enter into the equation. Instead, differences of opinion are battled on the basis of who can negotiate more effectively, who can lay the greater guilt trip or who can yell the loudest.

In contrast a Christian marriage may be compared to a very different organizational structure. The spouses relate to one another like department heads working for the *same* company. Christ is the boss. If one department head is in charge of shipping and the other oversees quality control, those two must remain on speaking terms. When a point of disagreement arises and communication breaks down, they cannot simply turn their backs on one another. The correct industry response is to kick the matter upstairs: together, they take their disagreement to the boss and say, "We've reached an impasse. You decide." And because they both acknowledge the same boss, they agree to abide by his decision.

So when we disagree as husband and wife, we recognize (for the good of the "company") that there can be valid opinions on both sides. We agree to let the Lord decide. And we wait until he makes it clear one way or another before we take any action.

This cannot happen routinely and effectively unless you and your spouse are practicing living in the presence of God. And it won't happen without a concerted (scheduled) effort to spend time in prayer, both separately and together. According to Psalm 127, "Unless the LORD builds the house, its builders labor in vain." Let's consider, in very practical terms, some of the building blocks of Christian marriage that relate particularly to a relationship growing in the aftermath of alcoholism.

1. *Agree on a purpose and goal for your marriage.*

When we counsel engaged couples, we enjoy asking them to define their goals for marriage. Usually they respond in terms that have little or nothing to do with a relationship between the two of them. "We want to have two children," they'll say. Or, "we hope to buy a house in three or four years."

Left unstated is any sense of what the prospective bride expects from her husband or what he anticipates from his prospective wife. We believe there is a tacit assumption most people make regarding marriage. It is a reflection of American culture today and bears little resemblance to the biblical goals for marriage mentioned earlier.

Without even considering any alternatives, people who opt for married life expect it to be a means of self-realization, personal fulfillment, a way to "meet our needs." That's not what marriage is all about. Getting married means taking on a totally new identity. In most cases it anticipates preparing a place in which children will be born and raised. Because two people love one another, they decide to share their lives. That is a valid beginning for a couple about to be married. But it is not enough.

If mutual attraction and personal fulfillment are the foundation upon which a marriage is built, how will it endure when trials come? How will it cope with the progressively more hideous behavior of an alcoholic spouse?

As we mentioned in chapter one, God's goal for marriage is simple: Two shall become one. Husband and wife need to bond with one another so thoroughly that nothing could split them asunder. Consider the bonding that occurs between a mother and her newborn baby.

Bonding with a baby does not occur instantly. It happens over time as the mother persistently (and joyfully) holds her baby, talks to him, feeds him, cares for him, scrutinizes him constantly. The new mother becomes a walking encyclopedia of information about her new baby. All you have to do is ask: "He weighs seventeen pounds and is thirty inches long; he drinks twenty-one ounces of formula every day; he likes his stuffed bunny and his red rattle the best." Is there anything about that baby that escapes the mother? Hardly. Bonding between husband and wife does not imply an all-consuming obsession, yet there is an important lesson in the example of the new mother. She pays focused attention to her little one every day and makes it a priority of her life to understand him and minister to him. If her baby happens to become ill, her attentiveness increases.

In a marriage ravaged by alcoholism, every goal or plan you may have dreamed of or shared probably appears to lie battered in the dust. Yet if you and your alcoholic spouse are in the recovery process, a new opportunity for bonding awaits you ... an opportunity that can draw on the strengths of AA's Twelve Steps as well as personal motivation and a realistic sense of new beginnings. Together you agree to help one another become all that God created you to be.

Exactly how is this supposed to happen?

2. Communicate meaningfully with one another.

You've set a goal for your marriage: to become one. And you've established a deep commitment to one another. The temptation at this point, particularly if you lead busy lives, is to put your relationship on autopilot. Even in marriages untouched by difficulties as challenging as alcoholism, the relationship will not fly for long if nobody pays attention to it. Communication is essential, and it takes work. There are said to be five levels of communication:

☐ Cliché ("How are you?");

☐ Reporting the facts ("It's so warm today.");

☐ Ideas and judgments ("I think . . .");

☐ Feelings ("I feel . . .");

☐ Total emotional and personal truth.

The fifth level of communication involves honestly exploring who you are, what you feel and what you stand for. In most relationships it occurs only rarely and usually requires a deliberate effort. Yet it is crucial to a thriving marriage relationship, and it really cannot occur between two people unless they have a close, caring, honest relationship.

In a Christian marriage communication at its deepest level happens naturally as you and your spouse learn to pray together for one another and for concerns you share. Prayer opens the door to honest, nonthreatening exchanges. And that, in turn, leads to closer bonding and more secure sanctuary in your marriage.

Invaluable practice in communication comes as well from participation in AA or Al-Anon. At those meetings, both the recovering alcoholic and the spouse can receive impartial evaluations from others in the same boat. Communication skills are honed as you are prompted to report on your feelings, actions and relationships. Techniques such as repeating back to a person what you think you heard them say assists in the process of learning to communicate effectively.

In the case of a recovering alcoholic it is especially

important to focus on *what* is being communicated as well as *how* it is communicated. For some guidance on this, Paul tells us:

> Do not let any unwholesome talk come out of your mouths, but only what is helpful for building others up according to their needs, that it may benefit those who listen.... Get rid of all bitterness, rage and anger, brawling and slander, along with every form of malice. Be kind and compassionate to one another, forgiving each other, just as in Christ God forgave you. (Eph 4:29, 31-32)

A home held hostage by alcohol is inevitably marked by damaging communications involving bitterness, rage, slander and malice. It is no easy matter to put an instantaneous stop to these established verbal patterns and habits. One way to begin is to decide to focus on the present and the future, not the past. Concentrate on seeing ways in which Christ is working in your life and your spouse's life, and let each other know what you see.

In our case this was very helpful. Dave's appreciation and regard for Elsie rose as he observed her growing in Christ. She became more self-confident, more willing and able to communicate honestly and less likely to clam up or just give in when a conflict arose. Hearing him praise her lifted Elsie's spirits and made a difficult readjustment to married life a delight instead of a chore.

One particular matter that requires careful communication is a decision the recovering alcoholic and spouse must make about alcohol: Should it be kept in the home? Should it be served to guests? Does the nonalcoholic spouse abstain completely for the good of the recovering alcoholic, or not? Some of the reasons why abstinence makes good sense are discussed in chapter seven.

In our case Dave abstains completely from alcohol always. For the first ten years after our remarriage, we kept no alcohol in the house whatsoever. After that, we agreed to keep wine and beer on hand to serve to guests and as a way to teach responsible drinking to our children. Today, Elsie drinks wine occasionally, and our grown boys drink socially as well.

Many recovering alcoholics and their families find it makes life easier if there is no alcohol on hand at all. And, as we outlined in the previous chapter, many Christians choose never to drink for reasons of spiritual and physical well-being. We are not proposing any "right" answer to this important question, but instead we encourage you and your spouse to come to terms with it together.

3. Anticipate conflict and meet it constructively.

In the best of marriages conflict erupts. There is nothing wrong with disagreements between spouses or strong feelings that are channeled constructively. There *is* something wrong, however, when a husband and wife hide their heads in the sand, pretending not to notice when the relationship breaks down. There is something wrong when you respond to conflict by seeking silent revenge or dredging up the past. By communicating well, you may avoid these traps. Yet there is even more to conflict management in marriages where either spouse is an alcoholic.

After alcoholism it is particularly important to determine ahead of time exactly what will go on between you if a disagreement occurs. First of all, make a covenant to pray together each day. This is a tremendous safety valve for marriage partners, because it is virtually impossible to pray with (and for) someone and remain angry with them. Second, memorize this verse: "A gentle answer turns away wrath, but a harsh word stirs up anger" (Prov 15:1). This verse summarizes a biblical approach to any sort of altercation. Finally, consider applying some of the following suggestions for settling disputes.

☐ Identify a quiet room or place in the house where you can discuss the problem uninterrupted. Once you've identified this spot, use it whenever a conflict surfaces. Don't let hurts pile up.

☐ When you talk, attack the problem, not the other person. Consider how you and your mate might have contributed to a misunderstanding.

☐ Back up accusations with facts. Ask one another questions to make certain you both agree on what you're disagreeing about!

☐ Keep the conversation in the present tense; don't refer to past hurts.

☐ Don't drag other people or circumstances into the conversation. Stick to the subject at hand.

☐ Speak directly. Tell your spouse exactly how you are feeling, and why. Don't make blanket generalizations by saying "you always . . ." or "you never . . ."

☐ Offer concrete solutions.

☐ To help regain your perspective and restore your relationship, ask each other these questions: Are we really disagreeing? Are we blowing this out of proportion? What do you suppose God is trying to teach us? How would you like to see this solved?

If you have lived with alcoholism, you already know that alcoholics do not fight fair. They escape into drunken silence, stomp out of the house toward the bar, or become so overwrought emotionally that discussion is impossible. When an alcoholic makes a commitment to recovery, he or she needs to learn basic skills of relating and communicating. By taking steps ahead of time to agree about how to disagree, you may pre-empt a replay of the ugly fights of your alcoholic past.

Marriage is a refining process that God will use to make us the best we can be. It means bestowing unconditional love on an imperfect person. It's a scary prospect at best. Yet it is an essential part of growing together—becoming one—in marriage. Several short AA mottos help remind us how to approach difficult moments. Sometimes the best first step in approaching conflict is to pause, say nothing and ponder these little sayings: First things first; live and let live; easy does it.

4. Stay in touch with friends who understand.

Alcoholics helping other alcoholics is the foundation upon which AA is built. The same principle applies to others caught in compulsive, destructive behaviors such as overeating, gambling and drug addiction. More and more, chapters advocating Twelve-Step programs to address these issues have been springing up across the country.

At the same time, a similar principle has been recognized among marriage counselors: Couples who are serious about keeping their relationship strong and growing benefit greatly when they develop relationships with other couples. In some churches, this goal is achieved through annual married couples' retreats or regular small-group Bible studies and fellowship groups.

If you are married *and* recovering from alcoholism, this

conclusion is inescapable: You need other people. It is asking too much to depend solely on your mate for support and encouragement or to be held accountable for changes in behavior that you have decided to make. Both of you will be healthier and happier if your horizons are stretched regularly by contact with other couples at different points along the road to recovery.

Staying married and improving your marriage require skills that can be learned. You could read books and watch any number of videos about marriage and family life skills, but real learning only takes place in the laboratory of life. By trial and error, by identifying people to be role models in our lives and by talking honestly with others about the process, learning is internalized and the skills are truly mastered. It doesn't require a great deal of brainpower . . . just a shared commitment and a belief that it is worth the effort. And it may mean taking initiative in your church or among other friends to develop the sorts of relationships that will accomplish these goals. It helps, too, to bear in mind that alcoholism is a disease that affects body, spirit and emotions. The recovery process is a long one. In one sense it never ends. Staying in touch with others through AA helps the alcoholic stay on course and avoid the temptation to drink. It is also the single most important factor in encouraging others to join the program and get serious about their own recovery.

When Dave met John L., many years had passed since John had taken a drink. Nonetheless, he continued to be active in AA, seeking out and helping people who were desperate for an answer that worked. John anchored Dave to the Twelve Steps and modeled, by his own behavior and participation, just how the recovery process works.

Staying involved in AA kept Dave from being overly dependent on Elsie, particularly during the second courtship and the early days of remarriage. When Dave traveled extensively on business, it gave him an instant point of identification in every new community. That is why after he was ordained and moved to Virginia, Dave kept up his identification with the group.

5. Take time to enjoy each other.

Finally, "going the distance" means finding in your spouse a lifelong friend. Working on your marriage relationship should not consist solely of effort and toil. It is important to relax and enjoy one another. This is the principle of "sanctuary" in marriage, which has been discussed earlier. It suggests protection, safety and peace, and it is an essential element in a lasting relationship. We have found that it helps to view marriage as a way of partaking in a grand adventure. "What is God going to do with us next?" Elsie and I often wonder. That question sprang to mind vividly after the birth of our twins!

How do you make friends with your spouse? We try to cultivate an approach to marriage that is based on discovery. No matter how long you have known your spouse (as this is being written, Elsie and I are approaching twenty-five years), there are always new discoveries to be made about one another. Discoveries can come during times of struggle as well as times of closeness and accord. Boy, did we ever learn a lot about each other during our extended blowup over country inns versus cheap motels!

We believe that in the marriage relationship you have the greatest potential for joy and for pain that you will ever have in your entire life. Being friends with your mate is one way to ensure that together you will experience more joy than pain. We have found that perseverance increases our joy. At the time of our remarriage, a nagging fear afflicted us both: what if things are no better the second time around, even if alcohol is not part of the picture? To our delight and (back then) our amazement, our relationship has grown ever closer, more playful and more filled with joy than we could have imagined.

It's not due to any special gifts or skills on our part. It's due to our individual commitments to make Jesus Christ King of our lives, as well as our joint commitment to place Christ at the center of our marriage. Viewing life in terms of God's perspective gives us an altered view of our importance and puts in perspective the world's compulsion toward self-fulfillment at all costs. Viewed in light of all eternity, the short time we're here becomes much less important. We can stop worrying about whether we're "winning" or "losing," and start focusing on what we can accomplish together while we are here.

Turning your marriage over to God may be a scary prospect, but it is a marvelously freeing decision. Here is a paraphrase of a short prayer we often use at couples' retreats and in marriage counseling situations. It offers a way of beginning the process of placing Christ first in your life and marriage:

Heavenly Father, we thank you that you are our God and that you love us even more than we love ourselves, even more than we can imagine. We thank you that you have a plan for our marriages that is beyond our wildest dreams. We pray we truly can get out of the driver's seat so you can lead us to experience marriage as you intended it—as the most fulfilling and most wonderful of all human relationships. Amen.

Rewards of "Going the Distance"

Throughout this book, we have emphasized two central themes. First, it is possible for your marriage to survive alcoholism. Second, it takes hard work and commitment to see it survive. As we conclude our chapter on "going the distance," we want to explore a third theme—one which we hope we have introduced implicitly along the way. It is this: Keeping your marriage together after alcoholism is tremendously rewarding. It is *worth* the effort, the patience, the setbacks, the doubts and the fears. Consider first the recovering alcoholic. The emotional and spiritual wounds of his disease are slow to heal and easily reopen under even mild provocation. In the context of a Christian marriage where real bonding and sanctuary exist healing can take place far more quickly and thoroughly than it would if the recovering alcoholic were on his own.

Damaged self-worth is restored when a spouse praises and encourages the recovering alcoholic, pointing out ways in which the person is changing for the better. And spiritual estrangement is relieved as the spouse prays with and for the person still struggling with the temptation to drink. Recovering alcoholics remain especially susceptible to peer pressure due to feelings of inadequacy. A spouse's active support might effectively counteract this.

In a marriage relationship the former alcoholic should be able to set aside personal doubts, criticisms or skeptical remarks that may cloud his relationships elsewhere and inhibit recovery. As he or she works through AA's Twelve

Steps, the marriage becomes a focal point for making amends, reviewing our wrongs and admitting them and learning how to live in a growing relationship with God. By persevering in the marriage, we believe the recovering alcoholic stands to restore wholeness and faith to his life to an extent that is not possible after divorce.

For the spouse who suffered through a period of active alcoholism, there are rewards as well. Usually, it is this spouse's choice whether to stay or go. As we have mentioned earlier, there may be ample reason for a trial separation, at least, and in some of the worst, most violent cases, divorce may be a sad necessity. Yet, for the most part we believe that even the most badly damaged marriage can survive and thrive.

The spouse of the alcoholic is rewarded with a well-deserved sense of accomplishment and relief when the alcoholic responds positively to treatment and AA follow-up. He or she has the satisfaction of maintaining family continuity in an age of far too many broken families and broken children. Going the distance means retaining important bonds of closeness between children and grandparents. It means modeling true, biblical commitment and unconditional love to your children and seeing them learn from it.

One way in which this aspect of "reward" came through to Elsie was in the form of a letter from our son Davie, while he was a college student. He just picked up a pen one day and wrote to her on legal-pad paper, saying:

You are incredible in my eyes. Your talents are quite abundant, as you may choose not to notice, but you constantly amaze me. I would love to meet the pre-Christ you and compare the former to the better. . . . What I'm trying to say is that I love you very much and care for you even more.

Finally, for the two of you together, the rewards of going the distance begin as you put in place "new structures" on the foundation of Jesus Christ at the center of your marriage. By purposefully developing a Christian marriage, you will each draw closer to Christ. In the process you will draw nearer to each other.

Keeping each other accountable as Christians and as marriage partners means you will begin to experience the fruit of the Spirit in your lives: love, joy, peace, patience, kindness, goodness, faithfulness, gentleness and self-control. These are the opposite of the acts of the sinful nature . . . the very traits associated with "drunkenness" and self-centered living.

When alcoholism threatens your marriage, there is a real temptation to consider the situation hopeless. That was exactly how we felt about it until God showed us a different path and a different promise. Our marriage keeps on getting better and better, and we don't quite understand why. What we know and affirm is this: God changed our lives, restored our hope in him and our love for one another, and continues to teach us what it means to become one in marriage.

Afterword

This book was written with two distinct purposes in mind. The first: to give hope to those caught in an alcoholic marriage. It often seems that the only way out, the only way to maintain sanity, is divorce. But divorce simply cuts off the relationship and leaves no possibility for healing or growth. When divorce occurs, you and your "ex" depart to find someone new, but you carry with you all the emotional baggage from the first marriage. In most cases, you forsake any opportunity or motivation to work through the problems, pain and character defects that developed during that marriage. That is why the divorce rate is remarkably higher for second and third marriages. When you divorce, you do not leave your problems behind; you take them along.

We cannot speak for every marriage, but in our case divorce was clearly the wrong path. We have found that by working through our problems together, we have both become stronger and better people. Our marriage now is stronger and more exciting than it ever could have been had we not gone through the fire together. That is why we have concluded that divorce is not the only way, and certainly it is not the best way, to deal with problems caused by alcoholism within a marriage.

The second reason for writing this book was to provide basic information to alcoholics and their spouses. This is not meant to be a definitive, in-depth study of the issue and all its physical, psychological and spiritual dimensions. Instead, it offers an introductory overview that allows the alcoholic and the spouse to begin to come to grips with the problem.

Because alcoholism inevitably involves a long and strong attempt to cover up the problem, any attempt at healing must begin with spouses sharing basic information. As such, this book is intended to be a resource for couples and counselors alike. We have woven this basic information into our story. We have attempted to share with you our feelings and how we applied this information to our situation. While reconciliation after separation and divorce due to alcoholism is extremely rare, it is our hope and prayer that it would happen much more often.

Frequently, people ask us, "Would reconciliation have been possible without the spiritual aspect of your story—without a commitment to Jesus Christ?" While theoretically the answer would be yes, in all practicality the answer is no. For reconciliation to occur, both individuals must change. Without placing your marriage on a new foundation of time-tested Christian values and principles, your attempts at reconciliation will likely find the relationship quickly falling back into old, destructive patterns.

In our new relationship neither of us is "in charge," and

neither one takes full responsibility for meeting the other's every need or expectation. We have placed our individual lives as well as our marriage in God's hands to do with as he pleases. He has promised that when people do this he will give them more blessings than they can ask or imagine. And he has.

This book is dedicated to Diane Gordon MacKenzie, my grandmother. I knew her as "Gamie." During all the hard times, when virtually everyone else had given up on me, Gamie never did. She always prayed for me and would let me know (sometimes subtly and sometimes very directly) that she expected God to do something with my life. I can remember waking up in the hospital in La Jolla, California, after a serious traffic accident. Gamie had come down from her home outside Los Angeles and was sitting by the bed when I awoke. I was groggy and I hurt everywhere. My jaw was broken in three places and I had 200 stitches in my face.

When Gamie saw that I was awake, she asked, "David, what do you suppose God is saving you for?" That one question has stuck with me all my life. Today I hope this book may be a small part of the answer. I have come to believe very strongly that if a person's life is going to change, very often there is someone in the background who prays faithfully for a long time. I thank God for Gamie.

Appendix:
The Myth and the Reality

1. Myth: Alcohol is predominantly a sedative or de-
            pressant drug.
   Reality: Alcohol's pharmacological effects change
            with the amount drunk. In small quantities,
            alcohol is a stimulant. In large quantities,
            alcohol acts as a sedative. In all amounts,
            however, alcohol provides a rich and potent
            source of calories and energy.
2. Myth: Alcohol has the same chemical and physiolog-
            ical effect on everyone who drinks.
   Reality: Alcohol, like every other food we take into our
            bodies, affects different people in different
            ways.
3. Myth: Alcohol is an addictive drug, and anyone who
            drinks long and hard enough will become
            addicted.
   Reality: Alcohol is a selectively addictive drug; it is
            addictive for only a minority of its users,
            namely alcoholics. Most people can drink
            occasionally, daily, even heavily, without

becoming addicted to alcohol. Others (alcoholics) will become addicted no matter how much they drink.

4. Myth: When the alcoholic is drinking, he reveals his true personality.

   Reality: Alcohol's effect on the brain causes severe psychological and emotional distortions of the normal personality. Sobriety reveals the alcoholic's true personality.

5. Myth: People become alcoholics because they have psychological or emotional problems which they try to relieve by drinking.

   Reality: Alcoholics have the same psychological and emotional problems as everyone else before they start drinking. These problems are aggravated, however, by their addiction to alcohol. Alcoholism undermines and weakens the alcoholic's ability to cope with the normal problems of living. Furthermore, the alcoholic's emotions become inflamed both when he drinks excessively and when he stops drinking. Thus, when he is drinking and when he is abstinent, he will feel angry, fearful, and depressed in exaggerated degrees.

6. Myth: All sorts of social problems—marriage problems, a death in the family, job stress—may cause alcoholism.

   Reality: As with psychological and emotional problems, alcoholics experience all the social pressures everyone else does, but their ability to cope is undermined by the disease and the problems get worse.

7. Myth: If people would only drink responsibly, they would not become alcoholics.

   Reality: Many responsible drinkers become alcoholics. Then, because it is the nature of the disease (not the person) they begin to drink irresponsibly.

8. Myth: Addiction to alcohol is often psychological.

   Reality: Addiction to alcohol is primarily physiological. Alcoholics become addicted because their bodies are physiologically incapable of processing alcohol normally.

9. Myth: Psychotherapy can help many alcoholics achieve sobriety through self-understanding.

   Reality: Psychotherapy diverts attention from the physical causes of the disease, compounds the alcoholic's guilt and shame, and aggravates rather than alleviates his problems.

10. Myth: An alcoholic has to want to be helped.

    Reality: Most drinking alcoholics do not want to be helped. They are sick, unable to think rationally, and incapable of giving up alcohol by themselves. Most recovering alcoholics were forced into treatment against their will. Self-motivation usually occurs during treatment, not before.

11. Myth: Some alcoholics can learn to drink normally and can continue to drink with no ill effects as long as they limit the amount.

    Reality: Alcoholics can never safely return to drinking because drinking in any amount will sooner or later reactivate their addiction.

12. Myth: Tranquilizers and sedatives are sometimes useful in treating alcoholics.

    Reality: Tranquilizers and sedatives are useful only during the acute withdrawal period. Beyond that, these substitute drugs are destructive and, in many cases, deadly for alcoholics.

Adapted from *Under the Influence: A Guide to the Myths and Realities of Alcoholism,* by James R. Milam, Ph.D., and Katherine

Notes

Chapter One: Alcoholic & Married
[1]Dr. James C. Dobson, *Love Must Be Tough* (Waco, Tex.: Word Inc., 1983), p. 90.
[2]Betty Ford with Chris Chase, *Betty: A Glad Awakening* (New York: Doubleday, 1987), p. 23.

Chapter Two: Hurtling toward Bottom
[1]Marty Mann, adapted from *New Primer on Alcoholism* (New York: Holt, Rinehart and Winston, 1981), pp. 20-23.
[2]Ibid., pp. 23-24.
[3]Ibid., pp. 32-33.

Chapter Three: What a Spouse Endures
[1]Morris Kokin with Ian Walker, *Women Married to Alcoholics* (New York: William Morrow, 1989), pp. 66-67.

[2]Marty Mann, *New Primer,* pp. 198-99.

Chapter Four: What the Alcoholic Endures
[1]Dr. James R. Milam and Katherine Ketcham, *Under the Influence: A Guide to the Myths and Realities of Alcoholism* (New York: Bantam Books, 1981), p. 62.
[2]Ibid., p. 65.

Chapter Five: Finding Help
[1]Vernon E. Johnson, *Intervention: How to help someone who doesn't want help* (Minneapolis: Johnson Institute Books, 1986), p. 104.
[2]Barbara R. Thompson, "Alcoholism: Even the Church Is Hurting," in *Christianity Today,* August 5, 1983, p. 27.
[3]Vernon E. Johnson, *Intervention,* p. 105.

Chapter Seven: The Alcoholic Parent
[1]Charlene Hoar, Ed.D., "Problem Prevention in the Now and Next Generation," in *Progress Notes,* a quarterly publication of Dominion Hospital, Falls Church, Va., Spring 1986.
[2]Janet G. Woititz, *Marriage on the Rocks* (Deerfield Beach, Fla.: Health Communications, Inc., 1979), p. 55.
[3]Charles M. Sell, "Sins of the Fathers (and Mothers)," in *Christianity Today,* September 10, 1990, p. 20.

Chapter Eight: Going the Distance
[1]*Alcoholics Anonymous* (New York: Alcoholics Anonymous Publishing, Inc., 1955), p. 123.

Resources

Books

Apthorp, Stephen P. *Alcohol and Substance Abuse: A Clergy Handbook.* Wilton, Conn.: Morehouse-Barlow, 1985.

Co-Dependency. A book of readings reprinted from FOCUS on Family and Chemical Dependency, compiled and published by the U.S. Journal of Drug & Alcohol Dependency and Health Communications, Inc. Deerfield Beach, Fla.: Health Communications, Inc., 1984.

Ford, Betty, with Chris Chase. *Betty: A Glad Awakening.* New York: Doubleday, 1987.

Hemfelt, Robert, Frank Minirth and Paul Meier. *Love is a Choice: Recovery for codependent relationships.* Nashville: Thomas Nelson Publishers, 1989.

Johnson, Vernon E. *Intervention.* Minneapolis: Johnson Institute Books, 1986.

Kokin, Morris, with Ian Walker. *Women Married to Alcoholics.* New York: William Morrow, 1989.

Mann, Marty. *New Primer on Alcoholism.* New York: Holt, Rinehart and Winston, 1981.

Milam, Dr. James R., and Katherine Ketcham. *Under the Influence: A Guide to the Myths and Realities of Alcoholism.* New York: Bantam Books, 1981.

Picard, Frank L. *Family Intervention.* Beyond Words Publishers, 1989.

Sell, Charles M. *Unfinished Business: Helping Adult Children Resolve Their Past.* Portland, Ore.: Multnomah, 1990.

Woititz, Janet Geringer. *Marriage on the Rocks.* Pompano
Beach, Fla.: Health Communications, Inc., 1979.
_____ . *Going Home: A Re-Entry Guide for the Newly
Sober.* Minneapolis: CompCare Publishers, 1981.
_____ . *Adult Children of Alcoholics.* Deerfield Beach,
Fla.: Health Communications, Inc., 1983.
_____ . *Struggle for Intimacy.* Deerfield Beach, Fla.:
Health Communications, Inc., 1985.

Organizations

Adult Children of Alcoholics
Central Service Board
P.O. Box 35623
Los Angeles, CA 90035
213-464-4423

Al-Anon/Alateen Family
Group Headquarters, Inc.
P.O. Box 182
Madison Square Station
New York, NY 10159
212-302-7240

Alcoholics Anonymous
P.O. Box 459
Grand Central Station
New York, NY 10163
212-686-1100

Children of Alcoholics
Foundation
200 Park Avenue
31st Floor
New York, NY 10166
212-351-2680

National Association for
Children of Alcoholics
31582 Coast Highway, Suite B
South Laguna, CA 92677
714-499-3889

Overcomers Outreach
2290 W. Whittier Blvd.
La Habra, CA 90631
213-697-3994